Endorsements for
Operation Olive Branch

Although Hannah likens her journey in these pages to her childhood friend, Nancy Drew, the title of this delightful book could easily be, "The Adventures of Hannah May," or perhaps something akin to Lewis Carroll like, "Through the Magnifying Glass!" My dear friend has created a clear trail through the wonderland of her personal journey to understand God's love for the Jewish people and the nation of Israel and to find her own special destiny within that great love. Thankfully, Hannah has made the trail simple and easy for us to follow, allowing her readers ease and enjoyment in learning the lessons of a lifetime dedicated to the God of Israel.

Marilyn Thomas, Director
Daughters of Zion

All through this book Hannah's sincere love for the nation of Israel and for the Jewish people is evident, yet all the more is her love for God and for His bringing forth the Messiah. What has delighted us as Jewish evangelists is Hannah's commitment to reaching God's Covenant people with the Good News that the Messiah has indeed come! You will read about individuals with whom she has had opportunity to share God's love. We had the joy of seeing this first-hand as one day she took us to a convalescent home where she introduced us to an elderly Jewish woman, Alice, who received Y'shua through Hannah's witness. So many churches today seem to have forgotten our Father's heart as written in Romans 1:16, but we are so grateful for servants such as Hannah May and for East River Ministries' support of our work to the Jewish people here in S. Florida. Inside these pages you will read "The Secret of the Blue M&M's," and will then understand how blessed we were to receive in the mail this blue M&M, with a stalk of wheat in his white-gloved hand – to represent a bountiful harvest for the Lord of the Harvest!

Michael and Mimi Finesilver (M&M)
Everlasting Life Outreach

As world opinion becomes increasingly anti-Israel (which is actually the new anti-Semitism), those who know what God's Word says about Israel and the Jewish people must make their voices heard. Hannah May makes a clear, pure sound, having felt the heartbeat of the God of Abraham, Isaac and Jacob for His Land and His Ancient People, the Jews. Her childlike faith, which propels her to act, is an inspiration.

I believe that God has called Hannah May to the Kingdom for such a time as this. I am also convinced that all Methodists, and Protestants of all denominations, would especially benefit from reading Operation Olive Branch, since God longs to bless those who bless His People Israel (Gen. 12:3).

Jamie Lash
Co-Host, Jewish Jewels TV Program

At its core this book extends a wholly gracious and eminently ethical invitation to the reader to come along as travel companion on a journey of discovery. Hannah May is one of those very rare individuals who truly understands that truth does its own work; you are invited, never coerced. This is not patched cloth; rather, it is a new garment. You will be intrigued by the majesty of the tapestry that the Lord has woven in and through Hannah's life journey. This book makes reference to several pastors and their own awakening to the revelatory truths herein. I am such a pastor who has been privileged and blessed in encountering the Lord's unfolding passion and urgent heart in this hour.

If you can stand it, you will be spiritually provoked, intellectually stretched, and foundationally changed as you intimately encounter Yahweh's passionate intent and desire for His chosen people.

Alan Ferguson
United Methodist Pastor

When we have a open heart to embrace the journey God has prepared for us, not only do we begin to see truth but God reveals His heart to us in a way that is amazing and life changing. Hannah May chose this way and was shown God's treasures and the beauty of His covenant plan for His chosen people. May we all be open to be a blessing and take part in this prophetic return of the Jewish people to their Land and their destiny.

Rev. Deborah Kellogg, Director
Cyrus Foundation
www.cyrusfoundation.org

I encourage you to find a comfy chair and get a cup of tea as you read Operation Olive Branch. I can only imagine that this is not the end of Hannah May's stories; it is only the beginning. Who would ever have thought that Hannah's violin; a sombrero, M & M's and jewelry would contribute to her understanding the mystery of Jew and Gentile becoming one in Yeshua? The final chapter of this mystery hasn't been fulfilled, but we have clues and hidden messages in the delightful anecdotes she has shared. As you read I pray that you join Hannah in her pursuit of unconditional love and support of Israel and her people.

Apothecary Cynthia Hillson
Precious Oils Up On the Hill
www.TheFragrantBride.com

Operation Olive Branch
A Collection of Mysteries
~Uncovered by a Spiritual Sleuth~

Hannah May

Energion Publications
www.energionpubs.com

Copyright © 2011 Hannah May

Scripture taken from the NEW AMERICAN STANDARD BIBLE® Copyright © 1960, 1962, 1963, 1968. 1971, 1972, 1973, 1975, 1977, 1995 by The Lockman Foundation. Used by Permission

Cover Design: Nick May

Except where otherwise noted, illustrations are by Nick May. Illustrations on pages xix, 51 and 138 are byMarylin Funchess. Illustration on p. 181 is by Garilyn Ferguson.

ISBN10: 1-893729-93-1
ISBN13: 978-1-893729-93-3
Library of Congress Control Number: 2011927462

Dedications

Just as my childhood hero, Nancy Drew, had a father, Carson Drew, that she worked alongside of to solve mysteries, I have a Heavenly Father who has invited me to discover and solve life's mysteries with Him.

To my Lord and Savior Jesus Christ, Yeshua the Messiah of Israel and the world. You have loved me always, and have taught me the meaning of the word grace, because You ARE Grace. I would never want to live without You. I want to be where you are always and forever.

To the great "clue dropper", the Holy Spirit, who keeps things fun and adventurous! It is a joy and pleasure to be taught by You. The Mystery Revealed: "Messiah/Christ in you, the hope of glory" (Colossians 1:27)

This book is also dedicated to my husband Greg, who has blessed me in so many ways. Greg, you have given me the freedom to discover who I am as a person, and to find out what God's call is for my life. You have sacrificed many things for my happiness and fulfillment. I could not do any of what I do if it weren't for you. Thanks for not minding if I do the writing or other creative things before I get the dishes done. I admire you and respect you more than you will ever know. You are a <u>real</u> Christian man and an example to many.

Acknowledgments

I want to acknowledge Greg, my husband here, but since the book is dedicated to him, I will let the dedication page speak for how I feel about him.

To Nick May, who is my youngest, but very grown-up son. I cannot thank you enough for all you have done to help me make this book what it is. I know I made you cranky at times, but I believe we have grown closer through this process, and I am so thankful that God has given me such a blessing to have worked with you on this project. Your many hours of diligent editing, drawing, computer graphics, and other skills deserve so much more that I am able to repay you. You are truly brilliant. You have brought me much pleasure as a mom, seeing the things you are producing and using for God's glory. And you are a daggum good writer. In fact, your writing makes me laugh and cry like nothing else I've ever read.

I want to thank Perry Dalton, whom I consider to be my father in the Lord, like Mordecai in the book of Esther to me. You continue to help me find courage and strength to fulfill this ministry of which God has entrusted me. Thank you for speaking into my life the things that you see God doing, and for drawing that out. Your life has had a profound ripple effect on mine. This book would not be a reality if it weren't for you. You have left a legacy.

To my Mom, Inez Russell, who has laughed with me and dreamed with me as I have walked through my Christian life. You have also listened to me ramble on for long periods of time, never growing weary of me. You have taught me by your example how to be a good wife, mother and grandmother. Thank you for loving me.

I also want to remember my dad, Roy Russell, who instilled in me a love for music and encouraged me to practice. He always said,

"Once this day is gone, you can never get it back." This has helped me in my writing as well.

Mary and Sid May, my mother and father-in-law, you have always been so good to me. Thank you for always being available and for the many ways you have blessed me over the years. Thank you for receiving me into your family when I was only a teenager. I had a lot of growing and learning to do, but you have been patient and loving.

To Anne Dalton, my other mom, who loves me unconditionally, and is always kind and patient with me. You have inspired me as I have watched your diligence and perseverance in writing and doing the things you are called to do. Thanks for accepting me as part of your family. Also thanks for being one of the people in my life that can make me laugh so hard it hurts.

To my son, Ryan: you are a unique gift of God with talents that are beyond the scope of my own imagination. You are a great listener, and have become a giver of very sound advice, and have done so many times as I have been walking through this ministry. I have always felt close to you because somehow, we understand each other. Your faith in Jesus is rock solid and He will always be your strength.

Benjamin, my oldest child, true to your name – "son of the right hand." I know I'm different, but you love me anyway. Your unique gifts, creativity and talents have blessed my life in many ways. I learn many important life lessons from you. You've listened to me, and seem to always know just what to say. God has used you more and more to alert me to things I need to know, especially involving my ministry. I love you so much.

Brianna, my beautiful daughter-in-law; I knew from the moment Ben brought you home, that you were the one I had prayed for all of Ben's life. I love the way you have encouraged me in my ministry, from the very beginning of our walk together. I also know that God has stirred you concerning His chosen people, Israel, and He will use you in whatever ways He desires, because of your willingness to serve Him.

To Ella, my sweet granddaughter, thank you for letting me share my heart for Israel with you. I will never forget our special Shabbats in my kitchen when you stayed at our house. Your Grangirl loves you so very much. You have brought beauty and joy into my heart with your smiles and hugs and kisses.

To my brother, David, who's exploits in the world of violins and Jewish things, as well as Kingdom things, are rocking my world right now! I look forward to the ways God will continue to connect us in the future.

Kayla, thanks for being the sweet and wonderful girlfriend to Nick that you are. I love watching you grow in the Lord.

Jody and Henry, you have made my long-time dream a reality. I have no doubt that you were God's perfect choice for me as my first-time publishers; and particularly on this project. All the conditions were right, and you recognized that and picked this thing up and ran with it. You are my friends, and I cannot tell you how grateful I am for you.

Pastor Alan and Garilyn, you have stood on either side of me many times, whispering encouragement and support to me. You have been so kind and gracious. I don't know what I would have done without you. Thank you for always reminding me of William Wilberforce who didn't give up for 20 years. I don't know if it will come to that for me, but thanks for the vote of confidence.

Dalia and Marylin, you have also been with me for years. We have shared a common bond, in our friendship with Sherri. We understand each other. We think much alike. I know you are always there for me, and I so much appreciate your love and comforting support. Dalia, we've been on a long journey of faith and friendship. I cherish you. Marylin, thank you for sharing your beautiful art with me as well as many others. It is making a difference. You are making a difference.

Iris, or rather, "Trixie", our walks with God have paralleled over the last few years in many ways. I marvel at the things God does through you. I would call them mighty for the Kingdom. You have inspired me in so many ways. You have taught me much about being real, open and honest with God. I love you bunches.

Verna, thanks for your love, encouragement, and belief in me and what I am trying to accomplish. Thanks for accompanying me on some of these mysteries. You had ring-side seating.

Alan and Judy, from the first time we met, we had a bond and a love for God's people. Your faithfulness and steadfastness has been a wonderful example to me.

Billy and Lisa Morgan, you are dear and special friends and have been incredible support for *East River Ministries*. Thank you for being part of the team, no matter what I was doing. You have always been right there for me. Thanks for your faithfulness.

Keri Uravich, we have been many miles together on this path of discovering who we are in Him. I think we are finally beginning to figure it out. Just so you know, my first realization of wanting to write came through you. Your gift of writing inspired me because it is amazing.

Shirley Hare, thank you for your countless prayers and intercession on my behalf. I know I keep you busy! It's so good to know that you are there, and that you keep me covered.

Angie, Nancy and Jeanette, thank you for always being ready to dance and decorate to be a blessing to Israel, and the countless hours spent in these activities as I've needed your assistance. You girls are incredible.

Lydia Spencer, Vicki Sigler, Linda Smith, and my cousin, Katie Morgan: You are four women whom God has used to mentor me at different points on my journey. I will forever be grateful.

A big thank-you goes to all of you supporters, helpers, and encouragers of *East River Ministries*, both old and new. You know who you are, but there are really too many of you to list here. You have all done your part in big ways and small, but in the Kingdom of God, things done for Him do not go unseen or unrewarded. I love all of you.

Last but not least, in memory of my friend, Sherri, who is with the Lord, but without whose influence my life would have been missing the incredible adventure that she taught me about. I hope this book does justice to both her dreams as well as mine.

Table of Contents

Dedication...iii
Acknowledgments...v
Foreword... xi
Preface.. xiii
1   The Clue in the Magnifying Glass.. 1
2   The Faded Clue in the Little Black Bible................................9
3   The Message of the Star Sapphire Ring 13
4   The Secret Message in the Necklace of Hope..................... 17
5   The Passover Mystery..25
6   The Mystery of the Old Violin...31
7   The Hidden Clue on the Gravel Road...................................37
8   The Mystery of the Two Abrahams..39
9   The Mysterious Wild-Eyed Woman...................................... 45
10   The Jewish Cemetery Mystery... 55
11   The Mysterious Word..67
12   The Secret of the Blue M&M's...73
13   The Search for the Lost Coin...77
14   The Message of the Open Doors.. 85
15   Hannah's Hanukkah Adventure..93
16   The Clue in the Old Library...97
17   The Clue in the Crashing Bookcase.................................... 103
18   Danger in New York City... 109
19   The Secret in the Wailing Wall.. 117
20   A Surprise Encounter on the Temple Mount..................... 127

21 The Mystery of the Dove in the Barbed Wire...................... 133
22 The Case of the Mysterious Poll-Taker................................139
23 The Clue of the Delegate Badge...145
24 The Hidden Message at the Fall Festival............................153
25 Clue in the Mexican Sombrero... 159
26 God's Mysterious Connections..165
27 The Twelve Tribes Mystery.. 175
28 Sherri's Secret Message.. 185
29 The Hidden Surprise in the Old Wesley Hymnal............... 191
30 The Note in A Bottle Mystery... 197
    Afterword..205

Appendices
A: Poll on the Middle East Crisis...209
B: Resolution Regarding Israel
    and Replacement Theology..211
C: Resolution Regarding the Jewish People
    and Anti-Semitism.. 213
D: Twelve Tribes Small Groups... 215
E: Hidden Items in the Cover Art...219

Foreword

Operation Olive Branch is intriguing as you are pulled from page to page looking for the next clue. It is delightful, inspiring, informative and life changing. If you are a Christian, it will give you a new appreciation for your Judeo-Christian Heritage. If you are Jewish, it will give you a new understanding and appreciation for Christians who love you because you are God's Chosen People. It will give to all a new appreciation of Israel and the struggles of the Jewish people to survive.

Operation Olive Branch is the story of the author's desire to be obedient to the Bible's command to pray for and bless Israel. Hannah May has been on a life long adventure, reading, studying and advocating for the Jewish people. Each chapter is a search for answers or guidance in this process.

As Hannah May's pastor for some 15 years I have watched the birth of *Operation Olive Branch* – several times having to rescue it from being aborted. I have accompanied Hannah on many of her journeys. I learned early on that no matter how foolish and impossible the situation might look, that God would appear in the middle of it and give it meaning and application. The wonderful part of the experience for me has been the process of mentoring Hannah, watching her grow up, watching a fearful young woman become mature, confident and brave, resolved to accomplish what God has called her to do – no matter the cost.

I challenge you to read *Operation Olive Branch* and discover Hannah's passionate zeal. Some of the vignettes will break your heart as you identify with Hannah. You will cry. You will laugh. You will pray. You will rejoice.

Sincerely,
Perry M. Dalton
United Methodist Pastor

Preface
Statement of Faith

The human nature in all of us has the tendency to want to make doctrine out of things that were never meant to be. Some things, besides the unchangeable foundational truths of our faith, can potentially become "another gospel" (1 Cor. 3:11-15, Gal. 1:6-7). For this very reason, I felt a need to express the main truths that I hold to, lest someone read what I have written, misconstrue my intent and make a doctrine out of it.

I believe that the moment a person (whether Jew or Gentile) truly believes and confesses that God, because of His love for us, sent His only Son to die for our sins, and then receives this free gift – he/she is eternally saved (John 3:16, Rom. 10:9-10). We must understand that Jesus, the Son, is God in the flesh – one with the Father and the Holy Spirit (John 10:30, Matt. 3:16-17). Jesus said that He is the way, the truth and the life, and that there is no other way to the Father but through Him (John 14:6). We are saved by His grace through our faith (which also comes as a gift from Him and has nothing whatsoever to do with our works). This is God's design to keep us from thinking we are better than anyone else, and that we can somehow earn his favor (Eph. 2:8-9).

I believe in the exchange of His nature for ours, which happens as soon as we receive His free gift and are made into a new creation (2 Cor. 5:21, 2 Cor. 5:17, Eph. 1:13-14). It is also an ongoing process that we could never accomplish on our own, but only through God Himself, who lives and works inside of us (Phil. 2:12-13). Being pure, being good and doing good deeds, in our own strength and power, does not save us (Rom. 5:8-10). Since we live in this body of flesh, we will spend our lifetimes being (outwardly) made into His likeness, sometimes getting it "right" and sometimes messing it up big-time. His love for us endures forever, and He will never leave us or forsake us (Hebrews 13:5).

He invites each of us into a love relationship with Him. This looks different for every single person. Others can inspire us, but we have to find our own way with Jesus by drawing near to Him and letting Him lead us in our own dance of life (James 4:8).

"There is going to be an outpouring
of which you have never seen before.
It will be as momentous or as important an event
as the joining of the east and west by the railroad
and the driving of the golden spike
joining the two together.
You will become a spigot for the United Methodist Church."

Word of the Lord through Pastor Byron Putnam
November 18, 2003

The Clue in the Magnifying Glass

When I was a little girl, every Saturday morning before piano lessons, my mom would take us to the library in downtown Pensacola, Florida. I would head straight to the section where the Nancy Drew books were, and then debate over which one or two books I would bring home that week. I could hardly wait to read them! I would get so caught up in the adventure of all of it. It always amazed me how those clues would materialize out of nowhere and lead her to solve the mystery!

Years later, when I discovered that the Lord was actually speaking to me, I began to realize that He operates much the same way. He would drop clues, and one thing would lead to the next until I had the answers to what He was revealing and what I was supposed to be doing to work alongside Him.

As a child, I always felt like Nancy Drew's life was full of adventure, excitement and amazement. This is how I really feel now, as an adult, about my life with the Lord! On another level, every trip I've made with God leading the way, every new adventure is like checking out the latest Nancy Drew book! Only now it's me living it.

God has used this mystery concept in a big way to lead me into writing this book. It has been revealed to me by hints, clues, people, scriptures, signs, etc. that I'm supposed to write it. The purpose is to share my own personal stories of how I have come into the understanding of things concerning Israel and the Jewish people, and what God is doing with them today. I am the Founder and Director of *East River Ministries*, which is all about loving, blessing and restoring the land and people of Israel.

Soon after I decided to write the book as a series of stories, at the suggestion of my former pastor, Perry Dalton, I realized I was going to do the book "Nancy Drew style," making it a collection of mystery stories. For the cover, I thought about having a big magnifying glass over the tree, magnifying the olive branch. This would emphasize the title of the book, which pictures the Jew and the Gentile, "one new man" in Messiah (Eph. 2:14-15), as the olive branches being grafted into the olive tree.

The adventure of writing this book really began when I received a package in the mail one day after I had already chosen the name and format for the book. My friend Marylin had no idea what she did for me when she sent me a Nancy Drew DVD as a surprise in this package of other items. She just felt that she should send it at that time. She had been frustrated because she had bought the DVD a while back for me as a gift, but for one reason or another was only just sending it.

Three years previously, we had laughed about how I likened myself to Nancy Drew, but we had not talked in the least little bit about the book I was writing and my thought to use a Nancy Drew theme. God's timing was absolutely perfect, to confirm to me that I was on the right track and that I had indeed heard from Him.

After receiving the Nancy Drew DVD in the mail, I excitedly wrote an e-mail to Marylin and told her about the book being called *Operation Olive Branch*. I shared with her how I knew that instead of chapters, there were to be mini-mystery stories. I also had not yet told her what had led up to this.

Earlier the same year, I stayed at a hotel in Montgomery a few weeks before Marylin had sent me the package. I was there for the 2010 Alabama-West Florida Annual Conference of the United Methodist Church, where, as a Lay Delegate, I was going to be presenting two resolutions I had written concerning the Jewish people and Israel, which would be voted on during that week.

I was looking forward to the time in the hotel that I could spend in prayer and seeking God about the week to come. God's clues on how to pray had been coming to me for a while; things concerning the history of the Jewish people in Montgomery, some of the Methodist history in Montgomery, pertinent scriptures, and other things that I felt were important for prayer points of focus.

The name had been chosen already for my prayer initiative, which was "Operation Olive Branch," and I had brought with me a piece of paper with this title, which had some of my research and information on it to help me stay focused.

I had written this up on a Word document and had put a picture on it set up just for the occasion. The picture had an olive branch alongside my delegate badge. Next to that was some Queen Esther anointing oil, which was made by a friend of mine, and the Brochure of Reports, which had the two resolutions I had written. I had arranged these items and taken this picture, simply as a visual aid, so to speak, knowing that no one would see it but me and maybe a friend or two.

Everything that happened in Montgomery happened before I realized that I was going to write this book. The clues began when I walked into the hotel. The first thing I noticed at the front desk was a large artificial olive tree! On the wall was a lion fountain. Lions always remind me of Jesus, the Lion of the tribe of Judah. Judah was one of the twelve sons of Jacob, and Jesus is from this tribe.

On the wall of the lobby, as well as on the wall when I opened the door to my room, there were pictures of the plant called, "Wandering Jew." I stood there in awe and amazement, because the plant in the pictures was just like the one a Jewish friend of mine had given me years before. The picture was hanging right over the little table where I would sit and work on my prayer initiative before I went out into the town of Montgomery to pray. That confirmed to me that I had indeed heard the Lord about what I was there to do, and that it wasn't just something I had dreamed up. He was right with me, leading and guiding and pointing the way and dropping those clues.

The best part was still to come because God did something else that was so amazing! My plan for the cover of the book had been to have a picture of the olive tree, because of what had happened in Montgomery. I then added the magnifying glass to the idea.

As I was sitting there looking at the contents of the box my friend had sent me, I glanced down and noticed the Nancy Drew DVD. I casually turned it over and noticed the description of the movie on the back cover. The sentence began, "With her magnifying glass…" and then I noticed that behind Nancy in the picture was a huge magnifying glass that I hadn't even noticed! That was really some confirmation to me that I was supposed to write this book!

I sat there for a while, thinking about the magnifying glass and the ways that God restores us, and how good He is. I suddenly realized I hadn't felt His presence like that in a very long time. I also thought about how I felt so much that I was walking in my purpose, and I realized the lengths God will go to affirm His love for me and for His people. I was truly amazed once again, as I sat there with tears rolling down my face, basking in His presence.

Later, I was typing a little letter to my friend who had sent me the DVD, explaining all that had just happened, and I signed it,

Love,

Hannah (Nancy)

Once again, I realized something else just as I typed the close of the letter. Earlier that week, a lady had written to me concerning my resolutions. In the letter she told me that her name, Nancy, is another form of the name Hannah! Both names mean "grace," or "favor." God is glorious! It is like I really am a Nancy Drew, hidden inside Hannah May!

We were still not done, however, with these awesome clues concerning the magnifying glass. God continued to confirm the theme of the book, in even more wonderful ways. I was in Pensacola the weekend after I received Marylin's package. My friend Iris and I were going to go to the top of the Pensacola Lighthouse that day, to pray over Pensacola, especially concerning the BP oil spill.

I had not told Iris anything about writing this book except that I said I was going to write one. I hadn't told her about the Nancy

Drew theme, although she was aware of my interest in those books as a child. When she came to pick me up to go to the lighthouse, I was in for another shock! We were about to leave and she said, "Oh, I've got something for you in the car." She went out and came back in with a big Nancy Drew album-type book and on the back cover there was a big – you know what – **magnifying glass**! I kid you not!

How amazing is God, to confirm this to me through two different friends within a couple of days? Now I knew beyond a shadow of a doubt that I was supposed to write this book, and that this was how I was supposed to write it. It was as clear as if I were a spiritual sleuth, actually peering through a magnifying glass at a big clue.

In any good investigative reporting, you must always have five "W's" and an "H." *Who? What? When? Where? Why?* and *How?* The important part of this story of the Clue in the Magnifying Glass are the *Who* and the *Why*. Who does the olive branch represent? And why do we need to know? The mystery of *Operation Olive Branch* could be misleading. Some further investigating will be required to get the true meaning of the book.

Many times, we think of the olive branch as representing peace. This is because of the story of Noah in the Bible, and the dove that he sent out after the flood. The dove returned with the olive branch in its mouth, as a symbol that the flood had receded and there was essentially "peace on earth" again.

Many people these days who are pushing the "peace process," "peace agenda," or "roadmap to peace," have used the olive branch to symbolize a peace that can come upon the earth as a result of negotiations. If you have watched the news, you have seen that there is an almost unspoken theme of "land for peace" in the Middle East. The Jewish people give up more and more land, and there will supposedly be peace.

We come to a closer understanding of the meaning of the title of this book when we think of the dove with the olive branch in its mouth as pointing to the coming reign of the Messiah, as spoken by the angels in the Christmas story. Every year we hear, "peace on earth, good will toward men" from Luke 2:14. This is how true peace will come, when the Messiah comes to rule and reign on the earth at His second coming. Jesus' first and second coming were prophesied by the angels.

Even this is not the main point of the olive branch, although it ultimately leads to the true peace. The symbolism for the meaning of this book is mostly derived from Romans 11:17-27, which was mentioned previously. The idea behind the title *Operation Olive Branch*, first for my own personal prayer initiative, and now for this book, is the restoration of the Jewish people, Israel, the original "olive branch" which was broken off for a time. In other words, for a while, it seems that Israel was set aside by God, so that we Gentiles, the "wild olive branch," could be grafted into the rich root of the olive tree, which is our rich Jewish heritage through Jesus the Messiah.

Ephesians 2:14-16 says,

> *But now in Christ Jesus, you who formerly were far off have been brought near by the blood of Christ. For He Himself is our peace, who made both groups into one, and broke down the barrier of the dividing wall, by abolishing in His flesh the enmity which is the law of commandments contained in ordinances, that in Himself He might make the two into one new man, thus establishing peace, and might reconcile them both in one body to God through the cross by it having put to death the enmity (the law). [my note]*

This is *Operation Olive Branch*. Restoring the Jewish and Gentile olive branches back into the olive tree, into "one new man," thus establishing true peace. We are His partners in the restoration process as we look at our history with the Jewish people and determine how to be used to bless and not curse God's chosen people.

Operation Olive Branch is about the Jewish people and the nation of Israel, and what the church's mission is in God's plan, as He reveals His mysteries. Much of this book is about what has happened as I have been doing what I could do, as only one woman, within my sphere of influence. Part of this influence is toward the United Methodist Church, and the other part is wherever the river of God takes me. It is my desire to help my particular denomination, the United Methodist Church, as well as all Christians, to understand why we should stand with the nation of Israel, bless God's chosen Jewish people, and pray for the peace of Jerusalem.

More and more, Israel and the church of Messiah Yeshua (Jesus) will need to stand together because of the fact that we have a common enemy. The anti-Christ and anti-Semitic spirits in the world today are working together to try and destroy the Church, (meaning the body of Christ), as well as Israel; however, as we can see in scriptures, the Lord has a different plan. We will all be one in the Messiah, which in itself is one of the greatest mysteries of all and is soon to be revealed to many precious Jewish and Gentile people.

Remember, these are mini-mystery stories, rather than chapters. Each one is an individual story with it's own message and can be read randomly or in order. Although they are in some sort of sequence, they are mostly unrelated, except for the overall message of the bigger picture, which is that we, as Christians, are to pray for the Jewish people and love them unconditionally as God fulfills His covenant with them.

Let's get out our magnifying glasses now, and become spiritual sleuths, uncovering together the mystery of the gospel of God's plan of grace for the whole world.

The Faded Clue in the Little Black Bible

I still have my little black Bible that I had when I was only 13 years old. It was given to me right after I got serious in my walk with God as a freshman in high school. The Bible has been washed, but you can still read on the back inside cover, in my adolescent handwriting, the very first scripture I ever wrote down because it spoke to me somehow. It was Romans 1:16 and it said,

> *For I am not ashamed of the gospel of Christ, for it is the power of God unto salvation, to everyone who believes, to the Jew first and also to the Greek.*

Little did I know, this would become one of my "life verses" that would come back to me later in life to confirm God's path for me. At the time, I wrote it concerning being a bold witness for Christ. Later, it would have yet another meaning, this time the emphasis being on the "Jew first" concept.

As a child, I didn't even know any Jewish people, at least that I was aware of. I grew up in the Lutheran church, but later in life, after the birth of my first child, I became Methodist. I chose the Methodist church because of the warmth I had felt while visiting my grandmother's Methodist church in Kentucky as a child. I came to love and appreciate the openness of the United Methodist Church to grow in your walk with the Lord from right where you are.

Early on in my days at a Methodist church in Pensacola, I began studying the Bible. I had an intense hunger for the things of God, and to know the Lord. It was in these Bible studies that I began to see that God was not finished with Israel. I began to understand that He had chosen them, and had made covenant promises to them concerning the land of Canaan (later to be called Israel). They had strayed from His path, and they had been scattered, true, but when God makes a promise, He keeps it. His promises were eternal and everlasting, and I could see that the fulfillment of these promises began when the Jewish people came back into their own land after being scattered for 2,000 years. The nation of Israel was

birthed out of the flames of the Holocaust, and now the dry bones of Ezekiel 37 were coming together once more.

My fascination with Israel and the Jewish people grew further when I discovered a program on TV when my children were small, back in the 80's. The program was called, "Jewish Jewels," and there was a Jewish man married to a Gentile (formerly Methodist) woman. They were both believers in Yeshua (Jesus), the Jewish Messiah. Every week, they would pull a piece of Judaica out of a treasure chest, and they would teach on that one thing, of how Yeshua fulfilled some concept in the Jewish religion. It was fascinating. This is where I first heard Romans 1:16 being put into perspective of how it related to the Jewish people. God has a Kingdom order and priority, with the Jewish people being His plan for the redemption of the world, because they would bring forth the Messiah. I had no idea that the "Jew First" principal would become my driving force in life.

It was somewhere during this time that I first heard and read the story of Corrie Ten Boom, the Christian woman in Holland who, along with her family, hid Jewish people from the Nazis in a little secret closet behind a panel of her wall. After reading this story, and seeing the seriousness of the situation, and how a whole Christian family had a vision to pray for the Jewish people, and were then called into life-risking action, it really hit home with me.

I could see that this was a matter that all Christians needed to take seriously, because what happens to Israel really does affect us. If Israel and the Jewish people were still on God's heart, then they needed to be on mine as well. Israel and the Jewish peoples' modern-day enemies are just as real today as they were during the time of Hitler, and these enemies also come against the Church of Jesus the Messiah.

We should really look more, however, at the spiritual enemies in operation behind the people who are against Jews and Christians. These people are operating under anti-Christ, and anti-Semitic spirits. We must always remember that our true battle is not against flesh and blood, but against rulers, powers, world forces of darkness, spiritual forces of wickedness in the heavenly places (Eph. 6:12).

It is through prayer and standing on God's word that this war is fought, knowing that Jesus has won the victory. His word places a priority for us as Christians in sharing the gospel with the Jewish people, as was written in my little black Bible from long ago.

The Message of the Star Sapphire Ring

I began to desire a star sapphire ring as I was approaching my sixteenth birthday in 1976. I really didn't know why, except that sapphires are my birthstone. I thought that a star sapphire was different and unique, so I asked my parents if I could have one. On my birthday, they presented me with my gift. It was beautiful. It was blue with a brilliant white star that would pop out brightly when it was held under the light. I wore it for years until I was married and had children. Then after my children were born, I had gained enough weight that it became uncomfortable to wear, so I took it off.

At some point, I went on a diet and lost a good bit of weight. Suddenly, I realized that my ring fit again. I began to wear it and enjoy it. One night, I went with my Jewish friend Sadie to her synagogue for a Hanukkah party. (The story of Sadie is told in "The Jewish Cemetery Mystery.") I dressed up for the party and wore the star sapphire ring. I had so much fun with Sadie that night, learning of all the Jewish traditions and celebrating this Jewish holiday, also known as "The Festival of Lights," or "Feast of Dedication." I realized that Jesus celebrated this feast in John 10 (beginning in verse 22), so I wanted to experience it as well. It was after I came home that I looked at my ring, for some reason.

The first thing I noticed, as if for the first time, were the colors. Until that moment, I had never even thought about those being the colors of the Israeli flag. Suddenly, the light hit the ring just right, and the white star became especially bright. It was then that

I noticed that the six points on the star sapphire were the exact same six points as on a Star of David. Suddenly, I felt something stirring inside of me. I went and got out my Bible and began searching for something, although I didn't know what. Finally, I found the words to Isaiah 49, and they were as if God were speaking directly to me. This became my call to ministry. The word said:

The Lord called me from the womb; from the body of my mother he named me. And He has made my mouth like a sharp sword; in the shadow of His hand He has concealed me. And He has also made me a select arrow; He has hidden me in His quiver and He said to me, 'you are My servant, Israel, in Whom I will show my glory' (vv.1-3).

Then in verse 5 it says,

And now says the Lord who formed Me from the womb to be His servant, to bring Jacob back to Him, in order that Israel might be gathered to Him, (for I am honored in the sight of the Lord, and my God is my strength). He says, "It is too small a thing that You should be my servant, to raise up the tribes of Jacob and to restore the preserved ones of Israel. I will also make you a light to the nations (vv.5-6).

I had studied enough to know by this time, that these scriptures were originally a prophecy about Jesus' mission, but then Paul also claims these words as his call in Acts 13:47 to bring a light to the Gentiles. I realized that since my salvation means that I, like Paul, am "In Christ," then these words can apply to me as well. In any case, the words seemed to lift off the page when I was reading them that night, and I felt that they were a personal word from the Lord for me.

I wrote in the margin of my Bible "two-fold ministry." I knew I was to do something concerning the restoration of Israel, and also being a light to the Gentiles (non-Jews), to help them understand why it is important to God that we, as the church, a nation, and a people, bless Israel and share the gospel with them, and how it has always been part of His plan.

The Lord called me, from my mother's womb, for this two-fold ministry. He put a desire in me to ask my parents for a ring on my sixteenth birthday that would remind me of His plan for my life.

The Secret Message in the Necklace of Hope

Over the years, there have been occasions when the Holy Spirit has prompted me to give something away. I'm not talking about something I didn't want any longer, but something I really liked. I will never forget the first thing like this that I can remember letting go of. At first, I didn't want to, and fought with Him about it. But then He changed my heart, and it wound up being one of the factors that set my path toward the Jewish people.

My little necklace with the Star of David with a cross in the middle was really a small thing for Him to ask of me. The symbolism of it, though, meant a lot to me as a young Christian who was discovering her Jewish roots, and this is why it was meaningful.

I had always said that the necklace was a great conversation piece with which to share my faith. Of course, I had many Christians stop and ask me questions about it, and "ooh" and "aah" over it, but I don't think I recall any Jewish people asking me, for obvious reasons, I suppose. I am sure many must have noticed this beautiful piece of jewelry, and just didn't say anything.

The message of the necklace was pretty plain. Jesus was Jewish, and I was a believer in a Jewish Messiah, which Jewish people have a hard time with, so unless they wanted to risk being "witnessed to," most would have never asked me about it. I'm not so sure that the necklace really had the effect that I hoped it would, but there was a purpose in that necklace that God used in a really wonderful way.

I was walking around Sam's Club one time, and I ran into a woman that I knew from my Methodist Church. I stopped to talk with her for a few minutes, when suddenly, she changed the subject of our conversation. Her eyes zeroed in on my necklace, and she said, "Oh, that is so beautiful and meaningful! Where did you get that?" I told her where I had gotten it, and she continued, "I really need to get one of those!" She went on to explain to me that she "really needed it" because her whole family was Jewish!

I hadn't realized that she was Jewish, because here she was, a member of the United Methodist Church. If, however, her whole family was Jewish, that would make her Jewish too, right? (Being Jewish is a religion as well as a nationality). Yes, she explained to me that she had become a believer in Yeshua/Jesus, the Jewish Messiah, and that her family wasn't happy about it. Her parents had cut her off, or disowned her, which happens many times when a Jewish person becomes a believer; in fact, sometimes they literally look at it as if their own children or relatives are dead to them. This woman had a lot of other family members, though, that she had been trying to share her faith with. So far, they had not become believers. They were not being convinced that Jesus, "the Gentile God" (in their viewpoint) was for Jewish people.

She said, "If they see me wearing a necklace like this, it will make more sense to them. I feel it would be a way I could share my faith with them." It was at this moment, that I felt the first little promptings of the Holy Spirit. He was saying to me, "Give her the necklace," so I began having a tug of war in my head and heart. I was carrying on a conversation with her outwardly, and inside there was a battle going on. I didn't want to give up my necklace; after all, it was a way for me to share my faith! I had told her where she could get one, so shouldn't I just forget about it? The Holy Spirit seemed to be showing me that it really could be a way for *her* to share with her Jewish relatives!" I had to admit, the Lord had a good point, but I walked out of Sam's with the necklace on.

I forgot about it for a little while, at least in my conscious thinking. I believe it was still there in my sub-conscious, waiting for the moment when the Holy Spirit would draw it back to my remembrance. That moment came when I was spending some time one evening, reading, praying, and studying. It was one of those nights I was trying to unwind after a long, busy day of homeschooling, cooking, cleaning, running to the grocery store, taking the kids to ball practice, etc. I had my Bible laying nearby, and I was reading a book and relaxing.

I happened to glance down and noticed the necklace, which I always wore. I looked down at the familiar Star of David with the cross in the center. In the quiet of my alone time, looking at the necklace closer, I heard His voice again in my spirit. "I want you to give her the necklace."

I began to argue with Him. "Its my necklace and I love it! I don't want to give it up." That argument only lasted a minute this time. I had already begun to think of how I would get it to her. I grabbed my Bible, and opened it and began to read. This is where the Lord sealed the deal and actually turned my desire to where I wanted to send her the necklace.

I was reading Isaiah when I came to Chapter 49. This was the chapter where He had given me my original calling at another time in the past. That was the time told about in "The Mystery of the Star Sapphire Ring," when the bright light hit the star just right, and popped out and I noticed it was blue and white. It was like the colors of Israel, and the star had the same six points as the Star of David. That had been in December of 1997, during Hanukkah, the Festival of Lights. This time, I kept reading until I got to verse 18. When I read this verse, it popped out at me and I was able to see the panoramic viewpoint of God about this necklace.

The verse reads:

Lift up your eyes and look around; all of them gather together, they come to you. As I live, declares the Lord, You shall surely put on all of them as jewels, and bind them on as a bride.

Suddenly, I could see what God was saying. My necklace was to be a seed. I asked myself, "What is a necklace, compared to Jewish people coming to know the Lord?" I felt that through this verse, God was speaking to me that the salvations would occur out of the "seed of faith" in giving that necklace to this woman so she could share with her Jewish relatives, would be worth so much in the Kingdom.

Each individual person who would see this Christian/Jewish woman wearing it would be one of those jewels from that verse. They could be touched by me letting go of a material thing that I wanted to keep, which was the necklace. It seemed that God was showing me that someday I would understand. These would be people who would somehow be part of the jewels in the crown that I would be able to lay at the feet of Jesus, as His bride.

The next morning, I didn't hesitate. In faith, I found the woman's address and put the necklace in the mail. I made some notations in my Bible; "1/8/98," "necklace" and "seed of faith." I didn't need the necklace as my reminder any longer, but I didn't want to forget this special night. God's word had been my treasure, my delight, my joy, giving me the hope of knowing that lives would be changed for the Kingdom.

This, however, is not the end of the story. I was telling this story to a friend of mine, who's name was Helen, not long after all of this happened. She enjoyed hearing how God had used this necklace to accomplish something for the Kingdom. Later, I was at a revival meeting, and went to sit next to Helen. She was waiting excitedly for me to arrive. She said to me, "I have something for you, but I have to go take care of the communion tonight. Can you follow me to the room where I am preparing tonight's communion?" I said, "Sure," and we took off. When we got into this little room, something like a closet, she excitedly told me, "Close your eyes, and open your hand." We were giggling like little girls. She said, "Okay, now open your eyes." I looked, and in my hand was a necklace, just like the precious one that I had given away!" We both jumped up and down with excitement. I said, "Helen, how and where did you get this necklace?"

Circumstances would have it that she had recently been in a jewelry store looking around for a gift for someone, or to purchase something for herself; I'm not sure which. She had looked into the jewelry case, and saw a necklace with a Star of David with a cross in it, like the one I had told her about! She got so excited when she saw it, and began to tell the lady who owned the jewelry store about my story.

She told me, as we were standing in the closet, that the lady had been so touched by what Helen told her, that she said, "Here, take the necklace. Give it to your friend." She wanted to replace the one I had given away! Isn't that just like God? He gave back something that was special to me. Maybe it was because I had given the first necklace away, or perhaps simply because He loves me. I can't take any credit for any of it, because I really hadn't wanted to give it away at first. He had to speak to me through His word and change my desires to give it away before I would do it, a testimony to how His grace works. *"For God is at work in us both to will and to do His good pleasure" (Philippians 2:13).* He moves inside of us to cause us to do His will, by the power of the Holy Spirit.

As special and meaningful as that was, that God would give me another necklace, I also discovered the joy of giving. It wasn't long before I had yet another opportunity to give my necklace away once again, in a way that was just as meaningful, and yet, this time it was much easier, and I did not even question God about it.

I was at a prayer conference one night for some young adult college-age people. I had been praying with some of them at the altar, when suddenly, one of our prayer-team members waved for me to come over where she was praying with a young lady. The girl had been struggling with an eating disorder, something that I had understood because it was something that I had struggled with myself. God had given me some victories at that point, and my friend knew that I was the person to pray with the girl who was feeling quite hopeless as she knelt at the altar. I knelt with her, and after our prayer, we spent a couple of hours or more talking that night. We shared our sorrows, hurts, and struggles. Through the course of our conversation, I found out that she had a deep feeling of sorrow and anguish for the Jewish people, which developed after she had done a project on the Holocaust in college.

22 The Secret Message inthe Necklace of Hope

I was sharing with her that the Jewish national anthem is "Hatikva," which means, "The Hope." We were talking about how the Jewish people were brought out of the fires of the Holocaust into the newly formed state of Israel. Through this experience, Hatikva was written, speaking of the hope that they had for a homeland of their own. In relating this to my new friend, we talked about the true hope that we have in Jesus. He is really the only hope of salvation for all, both Jew and Gentile. The redemption of the world comes through Him. I told her that He gives us this hope not just for eternity with Him, but that He has given us hope for today. We all have hope, when we place our trust in the completed work of Jesus on the cross. We can be delivered of whatever we are struggling. He is "Hatikva" for us, and He is "Hatikva" for the whole world. She grabbed hold of this newfound hope that He could deliver her.

The next morning, as the students were preparing to leave, I knew what I was going to do. The Lord Himself had put the desire into my heart to once again give away a necklace. I took her into a Sunday school classroom, and told her I had something for her. It was just like it had been when my other friend had given the necklace to me. We were both so excited. I told her to "close her eyes and open her hand," which she did. This time, the reaction was a bit different than when Helen had placed it in my hand previously, although just as meaningful. We grabbed each other in an embrace, and wept together for a long time. She was leaving the conference different than she had come, because she now had hope that God had heard her prayers for healing.

My friend has been through many struggles over the years since that special moment. She has had ups and downs, but she has seen and experienced much healing from the Lord. And mostly, she has never given up hope. All this was from a seed, which was the necklace I had given away.

For the Jewish people, the real "Hatikva" or (the hope) is in Yeshua/Jesus, the Jewish Messiah, who gives freedom and deliverance from oppression, through faith in Him. We, as

Christians, must offer this hope to them, as they begin to take their place physically on their own land, and most importantly, eternally, in their hearts.

The woman in the beginning of this story to whom I gave the first necklace, needed hope for her Jewish relatives to be saved. My friend in the end of this story to whom I gave the second necklace, identified with the suffering of the Jewish people during the holocaust, and had endured her own personal suffering, also needed hope. When the Israeli National Anthem "Hatikva" is played, in my mind, it has a double meaning. There is "hope" for the Jewish people to be free from oppression in their own homeland, but as we all, both Jew and Gentile, come to know our Messiah, there is hope for eternity.

The Passover Mystery

I can remember well when God began to teach me in very profound ways about how Jesus is seen in the Feasts of Leviticus 23. These are the appointed times that God gave to the children of Israel with which to worship Him and to remember His great miracles forever. One of these feasts, celebrated every year, is called Passover, and is the story in the book of Exodus, where God delivered the Israelites from slavery in Egypt.

The first time I can remember Him showing me the reality of Jesus portrayed in one of these feasts was on Passover several years ago. I had grown enough in my awareness of these feasts of Israel that I knew it was indeed Passover on the calendar. I was going about my business that day when I received a phone call from my mom. She was telling me about my nephew Greg, who was 33 years old, the firstborn son of my oldest sister. He had been diagnosed with a cancerous, inoperable brain tumor. It had already been biopsied and confirmed as cancer by two different doctors and two different hospitals. It was a very serious condition, especially because it was apparently inoperable and there was no doctor who would attempt to remove the tumor.

I called my sister to talk with her about it. She was, of course, very upset. I tried to comfort her, and as I did, I found myself telling her the true meaning of Passover. It was a truth I had recently discovered for myself, and wanted to share it to help her to have hope for her son's full recovery. That particular day, however, she could not be comforted. The news was still too real and too recent for her to be able to concentrate and really grasp what I was trying to tell her. However, what happened from this time wound up being a source of comfort and encouragement to my whole family for years to come.

I had been reading about how when the children of Israel left Egypt, God had required them to take a perfect, spotless lamb, and sacrifice it. They were then to place the blood of that lamb upon the doorposts of their homes. This was so that as the final plague occurred, and the Angel of Death passed over Egypt, the first-born sons of the Israelites would be spared, while the first-born sons of the Egyptians died. God did this to protect His children, in a literal way, from death, while he judged a whole nation whose leadership had held them in bondage to slavery.

Every year, on the 14th day of Nissan (by the Jewish calendar), the Jewish people celebrate this feast of Passover, while remembering how the Angel of Death had passed over them because of the blood of the lamb. I'll never forget how I felt when the reality hit me that **Jesus literally died on Passover** many hundreds of years later! He died on the very day that the Jewish people were taking a white, spotless lamb to the temple and its blood was being poured out. This was done every year in accordance with the command of God, a visual reminder of God's past deliverance. We now know that it also pointed to the Messiah Jesus, the innocent Lamb of God who was crucified for our sins.

I was telling my sister that Jesus, who was also age 33, the same age as my nephew at that time, was sacrificed so that the "Angel of Death" would also "pass over" us, who had received the free and eternal gift of God through Jesus, and His blood is applied to the "doorposts" of our hearts. I knew that my sister and her son Greg had prayed that prayer many years before. I felt that this would be comforting to know, as I was having a full-blown revelation of this truth as I talked to her. I believed that by her holding onto this in faith, her son could be healed. When Jesus died on the cross, He took the sins of the world upon Himself, and with that sin, He also took the curse of it for us. The Bible says in Isaiah 53:4-5:

Surely our griefs He Himself bore,
And our sorrows He carried;
Yet we ourselves esteemed Him stricken,
Smitten of God, and afflicted.
But He was pierced through for our transgressions,
He was crushed for our iniquities;
The chastening for our well-being fell upon Him,
And by His scourging we are healed.

As the year progressed, I continued to pray for Greg in this way. My sister's family continued to walk down the path and go through the open doors that God placed in front of them. One of those open doors happened when Greg remembered having seen a particular surgeon while watching a medical program on TV. This had been back during the time when Greg was just beginning to have headaches, and had not yet been diagnosed. The doctor on TV was performing a surgery on the same type of inoperable brain tumor that Greg was to find out, in the near future, that he had. Greg was able to track this doctor down later under some amazing circumstances. This doctor was the only one who agreed to attempt this surgery, when no one else would.

In the meantime, I was in the Christian bookstore one day, when I saw a plaque for sale. On the plaque was the scripture Jeremiah 29:11, which read, "For I know the plans I have for you, says the Lord, plans to prosper you and not to harm you, for good and not for evil, to give you a future and a hope." At that time I knew I had to get that plaque for Greg. I bought it, and mailed it to him, to give him encouragement. During that time, we also had many people praying for him. I can remember one night at our church, we had a healing service, and I remember going to the altar and our pastor coming by and anointing people. He asked what I needed prayer for, and I said, "Please pray for my nephew who has an inoperable, cancerous brain tumor."

The surgery was set to take place, and while Greg was in the hospital, before the surgery, God strengthened his faith with a small miracle. He and his wife were sitting in the hospital cafeteria eating together. He was naturally very nervous and concerned about his own situation; however, he looked across the cafeteria, and observed a young woman who was crying hysterically about something. Greg's heart of compassion went out to her, and for a few minutes, he forgot his own problems, as he prayed a silent prayer for her, continuing to look directly at her, but not moving his lips. He was praying in his heart that God would comfort her.

In the very moment that he prayed that little silent prayer to God, she looked up. Her eyes met his for a second, and suddenly, instantly, she took a little sniff, wiped her eyes and completely stopped crying! It was so sudden, that it took Greg by surprise. He knew in that instant that God does indeed hear and answer prayer. This gave him the confidence he would need, to know that God was answering his own prayers, and the prayers of others for him.

Greg had his surgery. The surgeon did remove a tumor; however, the amazing news was, that after they removed it and biopsied it again, there was no sign of cancer in the tumor itself! There was no sign of cancer anywhere! He would never even have to have chemo or anything. He was fine! Praise God for that. This was His miracle, considering the fact that this tumor had been previously biopsied twice and diagnosed as cancerous.

The part that is so amazing about this Passover mystery, and this is the *substance* of what He wanted me to understand about the Feast, is that the Angel of Death truly did "pass over" Greg. He was healed of cancer, in the way that God chose, so that He could reveal Himself to Greg in a personal way.

It didn't end there. It was really only the beginning of the miraculous story. **Exactly one year later, on the very day of Passover,** Greg's wife gave birth to their first child, a daughter. They named her Hope. Greg did not realize the magnitude of what God had done for him, though, until he returned home after his wife had their baby girl. He was in his house, and he looked across the room and saw the plaque I had sent him. The words sunk into him deeply as he read the words, "…plans for good and not evil, to prosper you and not to harm you, to give you a **future** and a

hope." Because of the Passover Lamb, Greg now had a "future" and literally, a daughter named "Hope."

The Mystery of the Old Violin

I took violin lessons as a teenager from a wonderful violin teacher in Pensacola. She encouraged me and jolted me, loved me and scolded me. I was on my way to a violin career, and most days after lessons, went home in tears, vowing to practice harder.

Then when I was 13, I had an accident and broke my left arm at the elbow. It was devastating, and for all practical purposes, should have been the end of my violin career. In fact, it was, for 18 years. After going through months of physical therapy, and trying to make a "comeback," I watched my younger brother surpass me on the instrument that I loved. I even attended the Meadowmount School of Music in Upstate New York for one month that summer. My teacher thought that if I could be taught under some very qualified teachers at this world-renowned school, possibly I would have a chance to regain some of my skills.

We realized that even though I had good instruction, nothing was going to change the fact that the bone in my left arm just would not ever have the flexibility it needed for me to be a professional. I finally threw in the towel. My violin was sold and I thought that was the end of it. Violin was always my passion. It was an instrument that I could play from my heart and soul. To lay it down was like giving up a part of me.

I was content after that to get married and raise a family of three wonderful sons. I was happily going about my life, not even thinking about the violin any longer, when the Lord waylaid me. Little did I know that He, the restorer of all good things, was about to not only bring my violin back so I could play for His glory, but

32   The Mystery of the Old Violin

was going to use it as I learned and grew in my love for Israel and the Jewish people.

One day, I was at my church and our Music Minister, Alan, was showing us a new video of Messianic Jewish worship from Jerusalem. Messianic is a term used for Jewish believers in Jesus. On the video, there was a Messianic Jewish violinist playing the most incredible music I had ever experienced. Not only was it lively, upbeat, and fun, but it was passionate, and soulful. It touched something deep inside of me. It was worship to Jesus, and yet with a Jewish flair. Suddenly, I knew I had to play the violin again.

All I could think about was owning and playing another violin. At the time, it was somewhat wishful thinking, because of our finances as a young family. God knew my heart, however, and for Christmas that year, my husband surprised me with a new violin. I can honestly say that was the best Christmas present I ever remember receiving. By this time, I had learned many, many praise and worship songs, and hymns, so I picked it up, and music just started to pour out of my heart onto the strings. I began playing in church and just in my own private worship time. At that point in my life, I didn't feel that I had to go and join the symphony; in fact, I didn't want to. I just wanted to play for Him. That's what I did, every time and every place the door was open.

In 2005, I was asked by my dear friend, Marilyn Thomas, to make a trip to Upstate New York, specifically for the purpose of playing my violin with a group of people who were taking a prayer journey. Sharon Springs was, for the most part, a little Jewish "ghost town" that was in the process of being revived. The town had been a summer retreat for many Jewish people for many years. After the Holocaust, in particular, many of them had returned there to bathe in the springs and bath houses. This was actually part of their repayment by the German government for the time they had spent in the concentration camps.

I had been asked by Marilyn, who was the leader of the group, to play a particular song, "You Raise Me Up." She said she wasn't sure why, but just felt like I needed to play that song during our prayer times. I had been listening to the song and practicing it. For her, the song spoke of how God raised us up to be closer to Him and how He helps us to soar and stand atop spiritual mountains with Him.

As we were taking off on the airplane and soaring through the air, naturally that song was on my mind. I had taken a book with me to read on the airplane. It was Jim Goll's, *Praying Israel's Destiny*.[1] As I was reading it and thinking about this song, something Jim was talking about in the book brought back a memory. He was explaining the concept of "Aliyah," the Hebrew families "going up" to worship the Lord in Jerusalem. He talked about how the fathers had led their families up to Jerusalem, singing the Songs of Ascent in the book of Psalms. I was taken back to the time when Sherri, my Israel-minded buddy, and I used to dream together. We always thought about how wonderful it would be if the men of the Methodist church would rise up and lead the way for the

---

1   Jim Goll, *Praying Israel's Destiny*. Grand Rapids, MI: Chosen Books, 2005.

Church to bless Israel. I thought about how fitting it was that I had been asked to play this song, which to me, and probably only me, meant, among other things, coming up higher in spiritual understanding about God's plans and purposes for Israel.

As my plane landed in Albany and I was walking through the terminal, I noticed that they were playing classical music in the airport. This was something that I had not heard in other airports. Suddenly, I had a flashback to the only other time I had flown in my life, when I was 16 years old. It was the trip to Meadowmount School of Music. The music that was playing reminded me of that previous trip, and I realized that this indeed was the exact same airport where I had landed all those years ago! I had one of those surreal moments, because I realized that I had been there before. I stood still in the airport, as I let God's Spirit overwhelm me, and I sensed Him whispering something to me. "Now you know why I brought you here all those years ago. It wasn't about becoming a great violinist. I was preparing you for your purpose and destiny. You are playing your violin now for Me, and for My people."

As I met my friends in the airport, I was overwhelmed with God's goodness, in realizing that nothing was better than being on a "mission" for the Lord. The first place we drove was the Jewish cemetery in Albany. We drove through, looking at the headstones with the Stars of David on them. Suddenly, we noticed a particular headstone of a young woman which had "stones of remembrance" laid on top of it, something Jewish people do on the birthdays of deceased loved ones. This headstone also had something else that caught my attention. It was engraved with a violin on it. Looking at the dates, we realized that *this very day* was her birthday, and that she had been 18 years old when she died. Her name was the same as mine, only a different form. It felt very strange to see this and we all felt led to get out of the car. Suddenly I had the urge to get my violin out. I began to play, there at the headstone of this young Jewish girl, in the midst of all the other Jewish headstones. We prayed for the families of these Jewish people who were buried here to know the love of the Messiah.

As we left the cemetery and went on to the little town, the sun was going down. For the last several decades, the town had been mostly abandoned and had gone into disrepair. There were many now empty and abandoned Jewish homes and synagogues. Some of the homes still had Mezuzahs on their doorposts. A Mezuzzah is the little box which contain the Torah, or Bible scrolls which are affixed to the doorposts. There was even a Mikveh in the town. A Mikveh is a ritual bath for Jewish people to do ceremonial cleansings.

After spending several different sessions in prayer in this town, we went to one of the small, quaint restaurants to eat lunch. I had my violin with me that day, and someone asked me to get the violin out in the restaurant and play. I was a little hesitant, but somehow it seemed like the thing to do. It was a beautiful fall afternoon, and people, who were most likely Jewish, were strolling by the window as I played.

When I play the violin, sometimes I am not sure what I will play next. I usually just play whatever comes out, and that particular day, what came out were songs that were from another time and place. One song was "Hatikva," which is the Israeli National Anthem, and the other was "Jerusalem of Gold." Both of these songs speak of the hope that is being restored for the nation of Israel. As I played in the restaurant, I felt as if I were playing over the town itself, as well as all those Jewish people who had come and gone through there. I was playing songs of hope and of salvation.

It was a surreal moment for me, as I felt I had come full circle. The violin that I loved so much, and had laid down for so many years, was now being used to play for the Lord in a way that was hopefully touching His people and bringing glory to Him.

The Hidden Clue on the Gravel Road

Two days after 9/11, I awoke from a very weighty dream. I have had a few of these types of dreams in my life, most of them having to do with my very specific call from God concerning Israel.

In this dream, I was on my hands and knees in Jerusalem, crawling on a gravel road. The gravel was big...I could feel the rocks under my hands and knees as I crawled. I looked down on the road and saw bloody footprints. I knew instantly they belonged to Jesus and I also knew that I was on the road that He took to the cross. I began weeping and sobbing as I crawled, following these bloody footprints. I followed them all the way to the foot of the cross. I looked up, sobbing. I had my arms around the base of the huge cross, hugging it and crying very hard. I looked up and saw that He was not on the cross. Then, I looked out beyond the cross, and I saw an incredible sight. As I watched, I saw a whole stream of children from all the nations of the world coming into view, each wearing his native costume, and carrying his country's flag.

The very first child was an Israeli child, carrying the blue and white flag of Israel. Next, was an American child, carrying the red, white, and blue flag, and right behind that one was a child from one of the Arab countries, carrying his flag. A whole string of children from all the nations of the world followed them. They were all coming in to form a circle around the cross, and I knew this meant that the people from all the nations of the world would ultimately bow the knee to Jesus.

When I woke from my dream, before I even had a chance to process what it meant, I reached for my Bible. I flipped it open, and just began to read these words from Romans 15:9-12:

> *Therefore I will give praise to Thee among the Gentiles, and I will sing to Thy name, and again he says, "Rejoice, O Gentiles, with His people" (the Jews), and again, "Praise the Lord all you Gentiles, and let all the peoples praise Him." And again Isaiah says, "There shall come the Root of Jesse, and He who arises to rule over the Gentiles. In Him shall the Gentiles hope."* [my addition]

I knew it was no accident that I was reading this. I realized this scripture confirmed that my dream was from the Lord. It was a visual of all the nations praising God, along with His people, the Jews, who were portrayed in the dream as being first. They were coming in to make a circle around the cross of the true Messiah of Jews and Gentiles alike, the Messiah Yeshua, who died on the cross for the sins of the world.

There has come, and will come, a Messiah, the Root of Jesse, who arises to rule over the Gentiles. The Word confirms it. The Jewish people, for the most part, don't yet recognize that the Messiah they are looking for has already come to the earth once, and is the same Messiah of the Gentiles, too. In the end, everyone will know exactly who He is. This dream is the "Jew First" principle, from Romans 1:16, illustrated. This is God's order, and it should be ours as well. When we put the Jewish people and Israel in our thoughts, words, prayers and actions first, then there will be fruit from every nation; people coming to know the Messiah.

The Mystery of the Two Abrahams

Another significant dream that I had was during the time of a great outpouring of God's Spirit over the city of Pensacola. The dream occurred on the morning of the first "Prayer for Pensacola," which was started by Rev. Perry Dalton at Pine Forest United Methodist Church, the purpose being to join churches together to pray for the city. I knew there was some kind of prayer event happening that night, but wasn't quite sure exactly what it was. I just knew I would be going, because I was there every time the doors were open in those days.

That morning, I had a dream that has literally influenced the course of my life. I dreamed that I was in a neighborhood in the East Hill area of Pensacola. It seemed like it was the 4th of July and that I had been at a block party or something. I was bored, so I decided to leave. I was walking to my car when, suddenly, I heard some very loud shouting going on. I was curious to see what it was about, and so I walked over in the direction of the shouting. There was a small, white, wooden house with a screened in front porch. On the front porch was a group of black people gathered having prayer. Their prayers were very loud!

I looked closer, and they were holding their hands extended toward the east, and they were praying for two things; they were praying for Israel, and they were praying for revival in Pensacola. They were holding up a large, white banner. On the banner toward the bottom, was a little garden. You could see the roots below the soil, and also the little sprouts coming up above the soil. Below the little garden were two words; "Seeds" and "Hometown," or possibly, "Homeland," I'm not sure which.

When I woke up, I sat straight up in bed and said, "Wow!" My husband, who was next to me, said, "You sit up the minute you wake up and say, "Wow?" I said, "Yes! I have just had an amazing dream! I'm not sure what it means, but I know it means something!"

That night, I went to church for the prayer, not thinking about the dream in relation to the prayer time, but when I walked into our church, I saw a whole row of black people there. I thought, "Oh, this is great!" We normally had mostly white people attending Pine Forest, so I was happy for the diversity.

We had several prayers, led by Pastor Perry and others. Then Perry said, "I want Willie Williams, Director of Top of the Bottom Ministries, which is a local ministry to help hurting people in Pensacola, to come up here and pray for Pensacola." I didn't know who Rev. Williams was, but when he got up to pray, I saw that he was black, and he was the pastor of the church that was with us that night. When he began to pray, he was praying in a very loud voice, and his congregation loudly began declaring, "Amen! Amen!" Suddenly, I was transported to my dream! It sounded exactly the same.

After the prayer time, I knew I had to meet Pastor Willie. I introduced myself, and said, "Pastor, I have to tell you about a dream I had this morning." When I finished telling him, he said, "Sister, that was not just a dream, but a night vision." I nodded my head, not sure what a night vision was, but I knew the dream was different, at least. I said to him, "I don't know for sure what the dream meant, but my initial thoughts are that if we want to see revival in Pensacola, or anywhere for that matter, we have to pray for Israel and the Peace of Jerusalem first." I felt this was the message of my dream, because this black congregation was praying for Israel toward the east, and also for revival in Pensacola.

I immediately began sharing this dream, and what I felt was the interpretation everywhere I went. I shared it with Pastor Perry and with Linda Smith, the Program Director at Pine Forest United Methodist Church, to all my friends, to the Sisters in Christ prayer group, and to anyone who would listen. I am sure they got tired of hearing me repeat that dream so many times.

I was a bit obsessed with this dream, and what it might mean. I began to research and look at old Pensacola pictures. I remember seeing in some of the pictures a little white church in Pensacola that had been there one-hundred years before. I wondered if maybe I had had the dream about the early "seeds" or prayers for revival in Pensacola that happened through a congregation of the past. Maybe we were to be the answers to their prayers.

I also began to receive understanding about the commonalities between the African Americans and the Jews. They had both had a Father Abraham, both groups had been mistreated, enslaved, in captivity, and had much prejudice against them. I did more research, and found out that the oldest Jewish cemetery was on the outskirts of town, in Brownsville. I felt drawn several times to go by that cemetery, which now sat in the very middle of a predominantly black neighborhood.

During that particular season of my life, I was often listening to Messianic Jewish music. I used to drive around the property of the cemetery, crying and praying for the Jews of Pensacola. I was interceding for them. I remember seeing a tree branch cut down on the ground of the cemetery, and I was crying out for Ezekiel 37 to be fulfilled, which was the vision of the dry bones coming to life, the whole house of Israel. (For more details on this story, please read "The Jewish Cemetery Mystery" chapter.)

This was also about the time that I began collecting pennies for Israel, and helping the Jews "make aliyah." I was a young housewife at the time, and one day, I was sweeping in my kitchen, when I noticed a penny on the floor. That day, I was tired, and rather than reach down and pick it up, I swept it under the refrigerator.

Suddenly, I sensed the Holy Spirit speaking to me about what I had just seen on TV. I had seen an infomercial about an organization that was helping poor Russian Jews to go "home" to Israel, which is called "making aliyah," meaning "to go up." I had just been wishing I had money to help them. "But, Lord, it's only a penny!" Then I realized that if I began saving the pennies, I would at least have something to send. Soon, I asked my church to help. We were able to help three Jewish people make aliyah from Russia! When I looked at that penny, I had seen in a new way, Abraham Lincoln's face on it, and it made for a visual reminder to me of the similarities between the Jewish people and the black people.

A couple of months later, we were at another meeting for the same "Prayer for Pensacola" which had begun to meet monthly at different churches. There were many people there, including a large group from Brownsville. I was so amazed when I realized that I was in a black church! It just fit with my dream, since we were there to pray for revival in Pensacola.

At some point, the leader asked if anyone had a word from the Lord for the group. My heart started to beat hard. I knew I would have share about my dream. I raised my hand and told them the whole thing. I was really hoping this group of prayer warriors would get it because God's message to me was clear by that time. "If we want to see revival, we have to pray for the Jews/Israel first." I even told them about Abraham Lincoln on the penny. They looked at me with blank stares. I got zero affirmation on that at all! I felt discouraged, but knew I had done what I needed to do.

On my way out the door, a beautiful, sweet black woman came to me and said, "Wait sister! I need to tell you something! I was totally with you, even if no one else got it. God revealed that to me long ago, even about the common 'Father Abrahams!'" I was so relieved that someone really did understand!

Since that time, I have constantly referred to that dream, and have tried to make it a priority to make Israel and the Jewish people first in my prayers. I am beginning to see a harvest of blessings in my life, I believe because of this priority. That penny I swept under the refrigerator, which gripped my heart, was the starting point for me to look beyond myself and make the Jewish people a priority. *East River Ministries*, which was formed to bless Israel, was born about ten years after this. Many thousands of dollars have now been given through this ministry to help and bless God's people!

Praise God! I hope that from hearing about these small beginnings, many people will begin to give the Jewish people and Israel an important place in their prayers and giving.

The Mysterious Wild-Eyed Woman

I was at my office at First United Methodist Church working, when a phone call came in to the front desk. I heard the receptionist talking to the caller. I heard the girl in the other room say, "She has to be talking about Hannah's pastor." At that point my ears perked up, and then the receptionist came into my office asking if I could pick up the phone and talk to the caller, because they had decided this person was actually looking for my pastor at Springfield United Methodist Church, rather than the pastor at First in Panama City.

When I picked up the receiver, the woman on the other end of the line asked me if I knew Pastor Perry. I said, "Yes, he is my pastor." Then she asked if I knew Sherri. I said, "Yes, she is my friend." She identified herself as a neighbor of my friend. She knew that Sherri attended a church in Panama City, but didn't know which one. She had randomly started calling churches and just happened to call the one I worked at!

Suddenly, I knew something wasn't right. She then went on to explain that Sherri's family had been missing since Hurricane Ivan. Their family of four had apparently flown out in their small plane and had not returned after ten days. I was shocked but did not know what to think at this point. She explained that Sherri's husband had not yet returned to his work after the hurricane. I decided to call and confirm. It was true. I talked to his co-worker who indeed told me that they feared for the lives of my friend and her family.

After I received the phone call, I then called the small airport where their plane had supposedly taken off. I talked to the airport employee who was there when they left and heard what he had to say. We just knew that the plane had left, but no one knew what happened to it. I was suddenly consumed with what had become of them, and what this would mean to my life and the lives of so many others.

I'll never forget the night I met Sherri in the late 90s. I was at Pine Forest United Methodist Church, my church in Pensacola. We had just finished a service, when this wild-eyed woman came running up to me. She said, "Are you Hannah?" I said, "Yes." She said that our friend, Linda, had told her she should meet me, because I had a love for Israel. At that time, I had been studying about Israel and the Jewish people for about eight to ten years.

Sherri had the most piercing blue eyes I had ever seen. She locked her gaze onto me and began to tell me this story about how some bread baked in her oven without the oven being turned on, or something like that, or maybe it was just that the bread rose in the oven. I do remember that the oven was off and, in her mind, something miraculous had occurred. I am now sure that she had connected the event with some Bible verse she had read that morning, and that is why the bread story was significant to her. God was using it to get her attention about the Jews, but I cannot remember exactly what the point of it was. All I know is that from that moment on, we were connected.

At the time of the phone call from her neighbor, Sherri had become a fixture in my life. Since we had moved to Panama City in 1999, she had become an Asbury Seminary student. She was traveling to Orlando every other weekend, and usually stopped in Panama City to come to the United Methodist Church where we attended. Our former pastor, Perry Dalton, from Pensacola, had been transferred to Panama City, and we had moved there because my husband was asked to come be the Youth Pastor. Sherri still felt like we were family and spent many Sundays with us.

She would come to my house after church, and we would spend several hours discussing Israel. Sometimes her children were with her, and they would play all afternoon with my children. Sometimes she would spend the night and we would sit up late and talk about all the things that were happening in Israel, and we would dream up ways we could be a blessing to Israel and the Jewish people, and we would pray for the peace of Jerusalem, as instructed in Psalm 122:6.

She had done more things for Israel than I had at that point, because I was more of a book person. I liked to stay home and read and study about people and places. Sherri, on the other hand, liked to actually go see the people and places. She went to Israel, New York City, Washington D.C. and various other places to pray for Israel and the U.S. Somehow, God always kept us connected, because the things He had been showing me in my studies would usually match up with the things she was actually seeing on a bigger scale in her travels and with her connections around the world.

The most important lesson I learned from Sherri was that we must take action and do something tangible to bless Israel, not only pray. It's not that I hadn't ever done anything tangible. I had already had the experience of blessing Israel through saving pennies, as I tell about in my story entitled, "The Mystery of the Two Abrahams." Sherri's dreams, however, were much bigger than mine had been. She talked about things like owning a huge ship, a plane, and cattle, all with the purpose of helping Israel. I tried to follow her. She was very difficult to understand sometimes. She was so out there with the prophetic vision that others could barely keep up. I was able to keep up to some degree, simply because God had ordained it so. There were enough key words in what He had shown me and what Sherri was saying, that we were within the same understanding about Israel.

Sherri was a mystery in herself. She actually had quite a mysterious and even complex nature that baffled many people. She had a way of repelling and drawing at the same time. The drawing usually overpowered the feeling of wanting to run away, at least for me. I was always amazed with her intensity of raw emotion that she had for Israel and the Jewish people, and also, her persistent desire to get everyone else on board.

48   The Mysterious Wild-Eyed Woman

There were times, however, when I couldn't absorb any more, and I would tell her so. I remember saying, "Sherri, I'm like a sponge, but I am full and nothing else is absorbing." She would take a deep breath, and say, "OK, I understand." That would last for about 5 minutes before we were off and running again. Some new key word would trigger a whole new round of discussions, leading to some action we *must* take.

One time, when she came to Panama City, we were having one of our deep Sunday afternoon discussions. Sherri and I both had a love for the United Methodist Church, but we felt that they seemed to view Israel from a completely different perspective than we had come to understand. She had just come back from a meeting with a rabbi, who had shown her a book that was about early Jews in America. In this book was some obscure paragraph that described John Wesley's sojourning with the Jews in Savannah, Georgia, as I described in the chapter, "The Message of the Open Doors."

Since Savannah, Georgia was where John Wesley, the founder of Methodism first came to America, she felt that we should take a trip there to do some praying for the United Methodist Church and the Jewish community. I told her firmly that I did not feel called by God to do this. However, she insisted that I was. I told her the Lord would have to confirm it to me if I was to go. She stood in my driveway to leave that day, telling me confidently to let her know when the Lord spoke to me, and that I had decided I was going. I waved good-bye; feeling assured that I was not going!

After Sherri left, I got into my car to go somewhere, and I had gotten behind another car. I glanced at the license plate, and suddenly, a peach on it grabbed my attention. I looked at the license plate. It said, "Georgia on my mind..." There were also other clues along the way that I was supposed to go, so I finally gave in and went to Savannah for quite an adventure!

Sherri's dreams about doing things for Israel got bigger and bigger, and it seemed that she always was drawing me into her wild ideas. It was not long before Hurricane Ivan hit that she called me on the phone to tell me that we were going to have a conference at my church in Panama City. She also informed me that we were going to bring the mayor of a particular city in Israel, and he was going to be the speaker. She was recruiting me to help her carry out something she felt called to do, and she was using her very persuasive nature to draw me in. This type of thing happened frequently in our relationship.

I said, "Sherri, how in the world do you expect to bring this Israeli dignitary over here? The cost would be too much!" She said, "Oh, no worries, I've got six-thousand dollars saved!" She was planning to use more of her inheritance money. Up till that time, all the money she had inherited from one of her family members had gone to bless Israel in some way. I said, "Well, what about security? You will have to have security for this mayor from Israel, and have a safe place for him to stay."

Then I asked her about the cows she said she was raising to somehow bless Israel. She had been talking about these cows that were on her farm for a while now, but she was feeding me so much other information at the same time, that I never fully absorbed it all. I seem to remember something about a beef jerky idea that she had to help Israelis in need. I said, "Sherri, exactly how many cows *do* you have?" She said, "Well, two right now, but I plan to have more!"

Then she said something that kind of made me sad. She said, "Hannah, you are really discouraging me right now!" I felt bad, but at the same time, I said, "Sherri, I'm sorry I'm discouraging you, but I'm trying to be practical here. You want to have a mayor from Israel come here. You are raising cows to make beef jerky for Israelis. I don't know, it all just sounds so far-fetched. I'm trying to be the voice of reason and logic!" We ended that phone conversation on a bit of a sour note.

A few days later, my conscience was really bothering me, so I called her. I said, "I need to apologize for giving you a hard time. You have such a great heart, and you have done more than most people to really accomplish what God has put in your heart to do.

Will you forgive me?" She said, "Oh, Hannah, I could never be mad at you." Then she said, "Oh, can I come down and see you next weekend?" I said, "Sure, but you may want to look at the weather channel, because there is a hurricane out in the Gulf of Mexico and they are saying it might come this way." She said, "Oh, I didn't know that! I will check on it!"

It was the morning of the hurricane, the day after my birthday, and the morning of the eve of Rosh Hashanah, the Jewish New Year. We had decided to ride out the storm, so while we were in our house, listening to the sound of the rain and wind outside, I was praying. I asked the Lord to specifically give me a word that would somehow relate to Rosh Hashanah, since I had been focusing on the meaning of this Jewish holiday while I was praying. I got out my Bible and my devotional, which was written by a man named Smith Wigglesworth over one-hundred years previously. I opened up to Sept. 15, and it was titled, "A New Day." The scripture reading was Isaiah 43:19, which said,

> *Behold, I will do a new thing, now it shall spring forth, shall you not know it? I will even make a road in the wilderness and rivers in the desert.*

I felt this was significant because of the fact that I had asked the Lord to speak to me about Rosh Hashanah, which is about new beginnings, and now He was showing me a scripture concerning Him doing a new thing. I wasn't sure what the new thing would be, but I did feel He was speaking.

I kept reading, and the devotional also referenced Revelation, chapter 21:1, 3-5 which read,

> *And I saw a new heaven and a new earth; for the first heaven and the first earth passed away...and God himself shall be among them, and he shall wipe away every tear from their eyes, and there shall no longer be any death; there shall no longer be any mourning, or crying, or pain; the first things have passed away." And He who sits on the throne said, "Behold, I am making all things new." And He said, "Write, for these words are faithful and true."*

Again, He was telling me that something new was occurring. I was relating it to the storm that I heard raging outside, but also to something deeper that was going on in my spirit, although at that time I didn't know what it was.

The opening words to the devotional were,

> See to it that today you press on with a new order of the Spirit so that you can never be where you were before. This is a new day for us all![2]

That day, after reading the devotional and the scriptures, I wrote in the margins of my Bible,

"Rosh Hashanah 2004 begins at sundown today."

"Jewish New Year - Day of New Beginnings."

"Jewish tradition is that God created the heavens and the earth (on this day)."

"Hurricane Ivan makes landfall in Panhandle."

Of course at the time I was having my devotions and praying, I had no idea that Sherri's family had left in their plane, much less knew they were even missing, and wouldn't know for ten more days. What did cross my mind that morning was how amazing God was to answer my prayer that He would speak something special to me on Rosh Hashanah. He spoke to me about "something new," and being that it was the Jewish New Year, it seemed so appropriate.

I thought about how awesome it was, especially since I seriously doubted that when Smith Wigglesworth wrote the devotional one hundred years previously that he had any idea about it being a Jewish holiday. Normally, the Jewish holidays fall on different days each year. Why would he know anything about Rosh Hashanah? Only a few Christians had begun to study and learn about the

---

1   Smith Wigglesworth, *Devotional*, New Kensingon, PA: Whitaker House, 1999.

Jewish roots of our faith one hundred years ago. In other words, I don't think the devotional, which was dated September 15, had anything to do with Rosh Hashanah, except for how it applied to me. God is so amazingly detailed that He can do things like transcend time just to make a point.

During that next week after the hurricane, it did cross my mind to call Sherri. (I did not know that by this time, they were missing.) I started to call a few times, but we were all so absorbed with the aftermath of the storm that I never did. Pensacola had received the hardest hit from the storm. When we realized that their plane was missing, the devastation from the storm made us aware that it might be difficult in particular wooded areas to even see their wreckage if their plane had indeed crashed.

The day I received the phone call from Sherri's neighbor informing me that they were missing, it was Yom Kippur on the Jewish calendar, the day that Jewish people were seeking to be forgiven for another year by repenting and examining themselves. They usually do a 24-hour fast from sundown to sundown. Even though as a Christian I'm not under the law, I decided to do the 24-hour fast and seek the Lord's direction.

That night, I was sitting out on my front porch, reading my Bible and praying. I believe that was also the night I felt the Lord touch my heart to write a book, which I am only now doing, six years later. The main thing I felt Him impress on me was, "Don't let this ministry to Israel die." Sherri had been going full-steam ahead at that time. She had been to Israel twice, and had plans in place for many things. Most of these things, I had no thought that I would have any ability to carry out, like having ships, planes, cows, or contacts with Israeli dignitaries, but I knew I could do what God had gifted *me* to do. God had made me different than Sherri, but the thing we had in common was our passionate love for Jesus and our intense desire to love and bless Israel and the Jewish people.

I said "Yes" to the Lord that night, to do whatever He led me to do, in the ways that were specific to me. All this was done not knowing for sure that Sherri and her family were with Him, although, I felt in my spirit that they were. Once I made that decision, I did not look back.

The next two weeks were very intense for all of us, as we tried to figure out what had happened to Sherri and her family. The police had come in and begun to investigate, since there seemed to be no trace of where they had gone. The air-controller of the small airport had remembered seeing Kevin, Sherri's husband, and had seen their plane as he prepared to leave. The problem was that a flight plan had not been submitted, so no one really knew where they were headed.

Everyone had ideas about where they might have gone, and why they chose to fly instead of drive, since their van was apparently loaded and ready to go, but no one knew for sure. Eventually, those investigating were able to find a copy of the radar from that morning, September 15, 2004. They were able to follow it until it read 2:49 a.m., and then it ended over McGee, Mississippi. The searching began there.

At one point, Pastor Perry, his wife Anne, and two other friends of ours, Dalia and Marilyn drove to McGee to the heavily-wooded area near the small airport where the radar signal had been lost. They searched as much as they possibly could through the woods, but were not able to find the plane. A couple of days later, search teams made the grim discovery, not too far from where our pastor and the others had been looking. It was confirmed that Sherri and her whole family had died. It was believed that it was an instantaneous death for all of them, so we realized that one second they were here, and the next, the whole family was in the arms of Jesus. We tried to comfort ourselves with the thought that none of them would ever know the pain of losing the others, since they all went together. The most comfort was in knowing without a doubt that they were with Him, because they had all trusted in the Lord's grace for their salvation.

Three different memorial services were held; one in McGee, Mississippi, which was centrally located for many family members to come, one in Panama City, Florida, where their church

54   The Mysterious Wild-Eyed Woman

membership was, and the other was in Molino, Florida, where Sherri's family had lived on their farm. It was a time that I will never forget, because of the impact it made on my life.

I thank God for Sherri. When I call her "Wild-eyed," it is in the most loving terms. There was something so lovely, so magnetic about her. When she locked eyes with you, you could feel the passionate heartbeat of God. People were drawn to her. I was drawn to her. She was part of me. I grieved when I heard that they found their plane, crashed in the woods of McGee Mississippi. Sherri had been used by God to change my life forever.

The picture of the bride is entitled, "A New Day." It was drawn and named by Marylin Funchess before Sherri's death.

The Jewish Cemetery Mystery

After I had begun my walk with the Lord as a young wife and mother, I was drawn into doing Bible studies at my church. In doing many in-depth studies, the foundation was laid for my beliefs on salvation, the rapture, the second coming, and also Israel. I could see in the Scriptures over and over that God was not finished with the Jewish people.

I did not yet know the term "replacement theology," which is the belief that the Church has replaced Israel in God's covenant promises and blessings, but I knew the truth that God had not changed His plan or His mind. His plan of redemption was to include Jew and Gentile alike. The Jews had been spread out all over the world into other countries, which is called the Diaspora, but had already begun to return to their own land, modern-day Israel, just as the Scriptures said that they would.

I began watching a program on TV called "Jewish Jewels," in which a Jewish man, who was a believer in Jesus as Messiah, was married to a Gentile (non-Jewish) woman. Their lives demonstrated how the two had become one in their shared belief in the Messiah. Every week they would pull out a "treasure" from their treasure box. It was a Jewish item, or something that would represent a Jewish concept, and they would make a whole program teaching on that one thing, and how it ultimately points to Jesus.

Overall, I began to gain the understanding that it was God's desire to bring us together as one in Him. I learned many things during that time, such as Jesus' Jewish name, which is "Yeshua." I also learned other basic Hebrew words like "Shalom," which means peace, and "Baruch," which means blessing. I even learned how to make Jewish recipes, like a noodle Kugel, which is a fruit or dairy dish with cinnamon.

I studied about Passover and how Yeshua perfectly fulfilled this feast as the Lamb of God who took away the sins of the world. I also studied about the Feast of Tabernacles. This is the time where Jewish people build a "Sukkah" booth in their backyards every year and live in them for a week, to remind them of God being with them in their wilderness wanderings. I found out that this was a picture of the future Millennial kingdom that is spoken of in Zechariah 14:16, which reads,

> Then it will come about that any who are left of all the nations that went against Jerusalem will go up from year to year to worship the King, the Lord of hosts and to celebrate the Feast of Booths (Tabernacles). (my addition)

It was very clear to me that the Lord Himself, the Messiah of Israel, will rule and reign in a literal kingdom in Jerusalem. In Christian belief, this is none other than Jesus in His second coming. These were just some of the things I became aware of in these years of study.

As a child grows during what is called the formative years, I also had my own formative spiritual upbringing. I developed a love for Israel and the Jewish people during this time that was very deep. I would get so stirred by Jewish music or reading a Jewish book, or watching *Fiddler on the Roof*! I began to have a yearning in my heart for these people, who were so loved by God, and who had been through so much.

I found out about all that they suffered during the time of the Holocaust, and I began to feel deep conviction over the fact that I had much German ancestry in my background. I wondered if possibly any of my ancestors could have been those who hated Jewish people. I lived in a state of repentance during that time, even though I had not personally done anything against the Jewish people. I just felt within every fiber of my being that I was so sorry for what had been done to them. They had been called "Christ killers." They had been banned from certain places and, of course, much worse. The atrocities of the Holocaust were too horrible for words.

I even found out that the man that I so admired for giving us the "faith only" doctrine in the 1500's, Martin Luther, was not kind toward Jewish people. Although he did the church a great favor during the Reformation, he had also wanted to share with the Jewish people the revelation about how we are saved through faith alone and not by our works. When the Jewish people still rejected the gospel, he said some awful things. He wrote books about them. One was called, *The Jews and Their Lies*, suggesting some terrible ideas about what should be done to the Jewish people for rejecting Christ's message of grace through faith. Apparently Hitler read this book and it was fuel for the fires of the Holocaust.

I can remember going to my former Lutheran church one day, and going in to talk to the pastor, asking him if he knew that many of the Germans had bought into the propaganda against the Jews. He looked at me like he didn't know what I was talking about. I'm sure he wondered why I thought it mattered now. All I know is that I couldn't shake the deep love and compassion that God had stirred in my heart for the Jewish people.

During this time, I had begun to play my violin again after not playing for eighteen years due to breaking my left arm. (This is told about in "The Mystery of the Old Violin.") Soon after picking it back up, I knew I wanted to play some Jewish music, but I didn't know where to find any. I called my former violin teacher, Mrs. "T," and asked her if she had any. She said she did not have any Jewish music, but knew someone who would. She told me about Sadie.

Sadie was a Jewish friend of hers from years before who had played in a local orchestra with her. Sadie had broken her left arm, just like me, and although I was now playing, she had never been able to begin again. Mrs. "T" assured me that Sadie would have some Jewish music.

I called Sadie and she invited me over. We became friends, going places together, spending time talking and getting acquainted with each other. She knew I was a Christian with a love for Jewish people, and she accepted me, just as I accepted her. She shared her violin music with me. This was the first time I ever heard of the "Kol Nidre," which is played at Yom Kippur in the synagogues. She gave me violin sheet music for it.

Sadie taught me much about Jewish life. I was fascinated by her menorah (candelabra) with the lion on it, representing the tribe of Judah that was from her father. I learned about the custom of lighting a candle for the dead in their memory on their birthday. I learned about the twelve tribes of Israel from a picture on her wall. She explained to me that she was a "Cohen" from the tribe of Levi. This was the priestly tribe from which she was descended. I was fascinated.

She even invited me to her synagogue one Saturday morning, although I, being a Gentile, would have to sit in the back section. That is the way it is arranged in the conservative synagogue. I didn't mind. I just sat back there and cried as I read along with them in Hebrew, trying to understand, and enjoying the beauty of the Hebrew language. Another time, my friend Judy and I went to a Hanukkah party with her and ate potato latke's with applesauce and sour cream. I loved experiencing the Jewish customs. It was that night I had the experience that I share about in the chapter called, "The Mystery of the Star Sapphire Ring."

She also invited me to a play at the Saenger Theater, called *Joseph's Technicolor Dream Coat*. She invited me because she knew that we would have a common interest in the play, since Joseph was in my Bible as well as hers. I remember that night, coming out of the theater, and it was cold outside. She put her arm through mine, and we walked together down the street to the car. I said to her, "You know, Sadie, we are like Ruth and Naomi in the Bible." She agreed that we were.

Ruth was the Gentile woman who joined herself to her Jewish mother-in-law. That was a beautiful moment that I will always remember. We also went to Krispy Kreme and she wanted to treat me to a lemon-filled donut. I don't know why that particular kind, but that was special to her, so I ate it. Now I always think of Sadie when I pass by Krispy Kreme, and particularly, when I think of the lemon donuts inside.

Another time, she invited me to a concert of Jewish music. She wanted to also invite her friends, an elderly couple who needed a ride. At the time, I had a big old Suburban, so I knew I had plenty of room. I gladly offered to go get them. What I had not anticipated was the fact that the man was crippled and walked with a cane and had very slurred speech. His precious wife was very short, and in fact, one leg was shorter than the other, so she had a platform shoe.

What transpired over the next few minutes getting them into the car was quite comical. We didn't know each other at all, so as they came out their gate to get into my car, I opened the door on the sidewalk as I introduced myself. The man tried to get into the car, but it was very difficult for him, because the Suburban was up so high. I offered my assistance, but he kindly refused. He eventually worked his way in, pulling and pushing till he finally made it.

I thought the difficult part was over, until I went around to the other side of the car with his wife. She hoisted her little leg up, but there was no way, it seemed, that she would be able to have the strength to pull herself up. I wondered if they would eventually give up and say forget it, but they didn't. She kept at it. Her husband offered a suggestion, although I couldn't quite catch all of it, because as I mentioned before, his speech was slurred. I did understand part of his suggestion, which was, "Why don't you try putting your butt in the seat first!" I couldn't help but laugh. We all began to snicker. She tried it, and then I remember pushing her in from the bottom of her shoes till she was within the inside of the car enough that I could close the door. By the time we were done, we were all laughing so hard it hurt! That was our first introduction!

The four of us went to the Jewish concert, which was a lot of fun. On the way home, the sweet little lady in the back seat began to ask me questions about my faith. She realized it was a Sunday night and I was still out with them, instead of in church. I said, "Oh that doesn't matter! I am doing exactly what I am supposed to be doing right now!" She said, "That is so wonderful! Thank you! Maybe we will just have to come to your church sometime!" Before I could get too excited, her husband began some sort of protest, but I couldn't understand him, although I still knew that she had been touched by God.

She told me of how she was in the hospital as a young person and a Catholic nurse had taken care of her. That was her first taste of the kindness of the Lord through another person. Those kinds of things stick. Some people plant seeds, others water them, but God causes the growth. That night, the Lord used me to water some seeds that had been planted. I felt very happy in my heart.

It was during this time that I was hanging out with Sadie that I discovered the Jewish cemetery in Pensacola. I was so fascinated by the tombstones as well as the gates with the Star of David's on them. I observed the Hebrew writing and the blessings and epitaphs. I saw the memorial stones, which were little rocks, on some of the headstones that family members place there on their birthdays.

Something about this cemetery stirred my soul like nothing else. At the time, I was listening to a new Messianic worship CD called *Adonai*, which had deeply soulful melodies. I can remember playing that CD in my car and sometimes just driving around the cemetery. I would be crying and crying and crying, thinking about all those precious Jewish people who had already died. I was also thinking about those who had not yet died. I wanted so much to tell them about the love of their Messiah. I thought of Sadie. Oh, how my heart yearned for her to know the truth.

I thought about Ezekiel 37, the vision of the dry bones coming to life. I had heard many ministers use this passage in reference to the *church* coming alive in their spiritual walk. While it *can* apply to the church, this passage is actually specifically for the house of Israel. There is a modern day fulfillment of this passage because the Jewish people returning to their homeland is, in a sense, the meaning of the dry bones coming to life and back into their land.

Operation Olive Branch 61

Verses 12-14 says:

Therefore prophesy, and say to them, "Thus says the Lord God, 'Behold, I will open your graves and cause you to come up out of your graves, My people, and I will bring you into the land of Israel. Then you will know that I am the LORD, when I have opened your graves and caused you to come up out of your graves, My people. And I will put My Spirit within you and you will come to life, and I will place you on your own land. Then you will know that I, the LORD, have spoken and done it,' declares the LORD."

What I was doing, I believe, was interceding. I was praying intercessory prayers for the Jewish people and their salvation. Pensacola has the oldest Jewish congregation in Florida, and

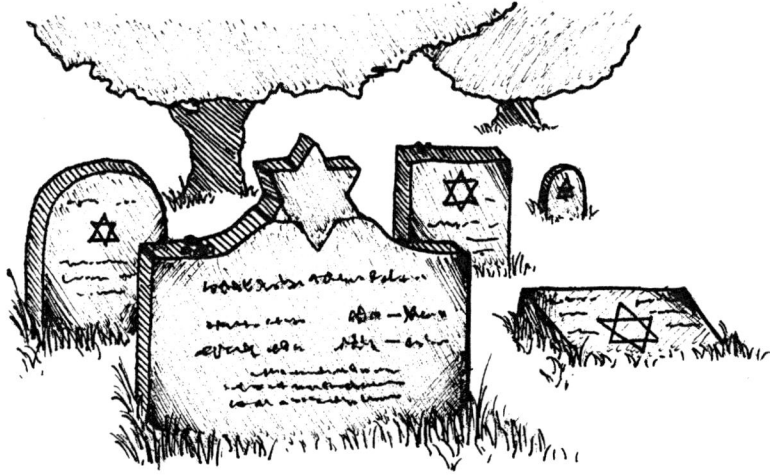

Pensacola is the oldest city in this country, predating St. Augustine with a colony which lasted for two years before it was destroyed by a hurricane. As I was praying around that cemetery, I believe that I was interceding for some of the very roots of Judaism in America. I was praying for all the buds on the branches that stemmed from these roots, who were still alive, who would still come to know their Messiah through prayers of Christians.

One day, when I was driving around the cemetery and praying, it was right after a storm. Many trees were torn down, and right beside the cemetery was one huge branch from a very old tree. Suddenly, I thought about the passage in Romans 11:17-26 which says:

> *But if some of the branches were broken off, and you, (Gentiles) being a wild olive, were grafted in among them and became partaker with them of the rich root of the olive tree, do not be arrogant toward the branches, but if you are arrogant, remember that it is not you who supports the root, but the root supports you.*
>
> *You will say then, "Branches were broken off so that I might be grafted in." Quite right, they were broken off for their unbelief, but you stand by your faith. Do not be conceited but fear; for if God did not spare the natural branches, neither will He spare you. Behold then the kindness and severity of God, to those who fell severity, but to you, God's kindness, if you continue in His kindness, otherwise you also will be cut off. And they also, if they do not continue in their unbelief, will be grafted in again, for if you were cut off from what is by nature a wild olive tree, how much more shall these who are the natural branches be grafted into their own olive tree?*
>
> *For I do not want you, brethren, to be uninformed of this mystery, lest you be wise in your own estimation, that a partial hardening has happened to Israel until the fullness of the Gentiles has come in; and so all Israel will be saved... [my addition]*

I thought, "A partial hardening; so that is why many of the Jewish people don't believe! They actually can't help it. There is a purpose in it. While they are not able to receive, the Gentiles are being saved; and then, those broken off branches will be grafted in again."

Romans 11:15 says,

> *For if their rejection be the reconciliation of the world, what will their acceptance be but life from the dead?*

I saw this partial hardening demonstrated in the life of Sadie. She was literally hard of hearing, not literally deaf, but in the sense that she was one of those who had weak auditory skills. She was much stronger visually. She loved to read. I noticed this during the time I spent with her. Anytime I tried to explain anything to her, especially of a spiritual nature, she seemed unable to absorb it. She loved to talk to me, but just couldn't stay with me if I were talking. I usually just let her talk, and I learned from her. It made me sad, though, that I was not really able to share the gospel with her in a way that she would understand.

It was not until I moved to Panama City, Florida, that I realized what needed to be done. We had not been unpacked too long in our new home, when I began to think about Sadie one night. I felt like something was unfinished. I had so wanted to give her the opportunity to hear the plan of salvation and how much Jesus loved her. As I was praying about it, the Lord gave me an idea. I remembered how she was weak in auditory skills, but strong with visual, so I decided to write her a letter.

I began to prayerfully compose a hand-written letter to Sadie, explaining God's love for her, and how we share the same Messiah. I made sure that I covered all the essentials of salvation through Yeshua alone, in the most tender and loving way that I possibly could. The letter turned out to be several pages long, but at the end, I sensed that the Holy Spirit had helped me to write it. I was nervous about sending it, but knew that I must. I didn't know if she would cut me off after reading it, but it was a risk I had to take.

I mailed it, and waited. I did not hear anything back from her. I was really concerned. A couple of months later, I went to my Mom's house in Pensacola, and decided to give Sadie a call. When she answered the phone and I told her who I was, she did not sound angry! On the contrary, she sounded welcoming and loving. She said to me, "I received your letter in the mail. I want you to know that it was the most beautiful letter I have ever read. I have read it over and over. There was just something about it that kept drawing me back. I don't know what it was, but I just loved that letter." I was so relieved. Inside of that letter, I had made it plain how to receive Jesus/Yeshua, the Jewish Messiah as Lord and Savior.

I felt like I had done what I needed to do. She had been so receptive to the letter that I had assurance that she had "received the love of the truth so as to be saved." It was not long after that time that I lost connection with her. I didn't know what had happened, and I had not shared that story with many people. Several years later, I met the rabbi from the temple that she attended, and he told me that she had died. I was sad, but I believe I will see Sadie in heaven.

Years later, the story of Sadie took on a new meaning. I had become reacquainted with my friend, Iris, after I had moved to Panama City and she to Georgia. I had not shared that story with her because at that time in my life, we were not as close as we are now. Later in life, we became much closer because we were so similar in nature. She often laughingly called herself Trixie Beldon, another mystery story character from childhood, which complimented my Nancy Drew personality. However, many years later, the Lord brought the fullness of it back around to me in a very profound way.

Iris also has a love for the Jewish people, and also has felt that she has some Jewish genealogy in her background. She knew what her mother's maiden name was, and she had researched it and found the name in a Jewish cemetery in New York City.

One day, many years later, she was over at St. Michael's cemetery for some reason. This is a very old Catholic cemetery in Pensacola, which is actually a tourist attraction. As she was walking around, she noticed that there were some Jewish headstones there. She thought to herself that this was a "picture" of the "one new man" from Ephesians 2:14-15, as there were Christians and Jews buried together in the same cemetery. The scripture says,

> *For He Himself is our peace, who made both groups into one, and broke down the barrier of the dividing wall, by abolishing His flesh the enmity, which is the Law of commandments contained in ordinances, that in Himself He might make the two in to one new man, thus establishing peace.*

It was just a little prophetic reminder to her that we are all one in the Messiah, although in the natural, that may or may not have been true of those individuals buried there.

As usual with Iris when she is in "Trixie Beldon mode," one thing led to another, and she wound up that same day going over to the Jewish cemetery. As she was walking around looking at the headstones, a particular headstone caught her attention because of the maiden name of a particular person buried there. The maiden name of the person was just one letter off from her mother's Jewish maiden name. When she got home, she immediately wrote me of her experience of finding this headstone of a Jewish woman who's maiden name was almost the same as her mother's. She had actually taken a picture of the headstone which had the small remembrance stones on top that some family members had left there.

She was excited about finding the name similarity, which was the reason for her call, but when she told me the name, I was blown away. It was Sadie. My Sadie. The one for whom I had prayed and spent much time, and had written the letter telling her of the love of her Savior, that she had received. What were the chances that of all the names on the tombstones in the Jewish Cemetery, that she would stumble across the one that meant the most to me? When I told Iris the story of Sadie, at that point we were both just awestruck at the awesomeness of our God.

This is how God works. He brings things back around full circle. I have visited Sadie's grave since that time. And now, when I look at her headstone, I do not feel that mourning and grieving, because I believe she heard the gospel through the letter. I believe that I will see her in Heaven and we will worship our Messiah together.

The Mysterious Word

I remember the day Pastor Mike from Kenya visited my *East River Ministries* office upstairs at Springfield United Methodist Church. As we were ascending up the stairs, I asked him if he knew what "aliyah" meant. He said he did not. I said, "It means, *to go up*." I told him that aliyah is when the Jewish people go back to live in the land of Israel. I shared with him my insight about how it is also a spiritual thing, that as we draw closer to God, we come up higher, so to speak. We have more understanding of a spiritual matter. He said, "Oh! OK! Now I see!" He really did seem to get it.

I opened the door to the *East River Ministries* office and he was amazed by what he experienced. God's holy presence was in the room, as it always seemed to be. I told him that this room was in this church specifically to bless and pray for Israel, a unique thing for a United Methodist Church.

I gave him a little pin that had an Israel flag and an American flag on it. He loved it. He had said earlier in Sunday school that in Africa, in his church, the only places that his people ever want to go is America and Israel. This is because of the *Jesus* film and because they want to see America where the Christians live and Israel where Jesus lived.

Later, during the church service, when he got up to preach, Pastor Michael made a point to say how awesome it was to see that we had an entire room set apart just to bless Israel. He talked about how important it was and how we have been blessed as a nation because we have blessed Israel.

Pastor Mike made a "spiritual aliyah" that day, in the sense that his eyes were opened and he got the understanding about the importance of Israel when he walked through that *East River Ministries* room.

This is exactly what I had envisioned when I first was given permission to have that office in the church. When I knew that I was going to carry on the ministry after my friend Sherri's death, as I tell about in "The Mystery of the Wild-Eyed Woman," I asked her family as they were going through her things if they would save anything for me that had to do with the ministry. I didn't know if they would, because we were strangers to each other, but they did. When God had shown me it was the proper time, I went and got her things, and brought them up there to have the office decorated with them.

The office was situated in a new upstairs part of the building, in a room that was intended to have a dressing area for the boys and men for when they get baptized. I knew I would not be in the office during any time that they would be getting baptized on a Sunday morning, so it was not a problem. And I felt that it was quite prophetic. Picture this. As they would ascend up the stairs on their way to get ready for their baptism, they would "go up" the stairs and walk right through the room that was a representation of Israel. Although it never quite happened that way because the dressing area was never finished, my prayer had always been that whoever came into that room would have a "spiritual aliyah" and have their eyes opened concerning what their part is in loving, blessing, helping and praying for Israel. Since that time, the Lord has brought people from several nations through there, and I have prayed that they would take the vision for Israel with them back to their homelands.

Sherri had a huge vision! She had always talked about seeing the United Methodist Church, beginning with the men, (who are the husbands, fathers and leaders), to rise up and take their places and lead the way with the rest of the church in helping Israel. She hoped that this would cause a huge turning of the tide within the Methodist church, which would ultimately affect the world. For many years, it has been mostly women leading in the churches, but

God has also gifted men to lead. It is particularly encouraging to see a man who is a leader in blessing Israel. If a man, a woman, or even a child can grasp the concept of the gospel being for the Jew first (Romans 1:16), it sets things in a "Kingdom order" so that everything flows the way it's supposed to.

Just imagine! If a huge amount of the resources available within the United Methodist denomination were to be released to bless Israel, what a blessing there would be that would come upon the denomination! Genesis 12:3 says, "I will bless those who bless you, and curse those who curse you." For whatever reason, Sherri always hoped that the men would understand this concept first, and then bring the rest of the church along.

About one week before Pastor Mike had come upstairs that day and had his Israel revelation, I had been prayed over by my pastor, Perry Dalton, on November 22, 2005. This was exactly two years to the day after Sherri had prayed a prayer over Pastor Perry during the *In the Shadow of His Presence Conference* in 2003. Her prayer over him had been concerning the United Methodist Church and Israel.

As Pastor Perry was praying for me that day, a couple of really memorable things happened. First, he prayed, "Father, may her life be an investment that brings forth much fruit. Father, when we speak of fruit, Lord, you know the fruit of individuals, but You also know the fruit of nations. And Father, I speak the fruit of the nations." This was very significant to me because I knew this would happen as I continued to lift up Israel first in my prayers.

The second thing that happened was that there had been a Paul Wilbur CD playing during the prayer. Just as Paul sang the words, "Come and take your place on your throne Jerusalem," (Jeremiah 3:17) suddenly I heard a train whistle blowing outside at that precise moment! Up to that point, the prayer had been more of a blessing for me. But at the very moment Pastor Perry said, "Father, we pray for the peace of Jerusalem," the train whistle blew! That would not mean anything to anyone, unless they knew Sherri.

Sherri had always thought of trains as symbolic of being used to help the Jewish people. Trains had been used to take the Jews to concentration camps and to their deaths, but she wanted to reverse that image, preferring to think of trains as the church walking together in unity, and in interdependence with the people of Israel, holding together God's purposes in His holy word.

When the train whistle blew during the prayer that day my pastor was praying over me, I was in a state of sheer joy and delight. I began laughing during the prayer. Not in a disrespectful way, but in a way that was so wonderfully full of bliss! It was a Holy Spirit moment like I had not ever encountered before.

During this powerful moment of prayer, my pastor then prayed, "Father, may many Jews make aliyah, because Hannah is out there cheering them on!"

And that is my desire. That many of us would be able to help the Jewish people make aliyah, or return to their land, as the Bible says will happen. In fact, it has been happening since before 1948 when Israel became a nation. The Jewish people who were scattered all over the world are now returning in a steady stream.

This was not the first time I had heard the train whistle blow at a strategic moment. When I had gone to Pensacola during a Feast of Tabernacles celebration, and had arranged to pick up the six bagfuls of Sherri's ministry things, there was a group of her friends praying about the future of the ministry. Suddenly we all heard a train whistle blow! We were all astounded.

It is also important to mention another connection concerning a proclamation Sherri had made in Israel. She had gone to Israel twice before she died. On one of these trips, she went through Hezekiah's tunnel, which is somewhat of a tourist attraction. Although groups of people go through the tunnel every day, it was a powerful moment for her, as she relayed to me later.

She had gone through the tunnel in knee-deep water, with a group of children in front of her, and there were men, Israeli soldiers, behind her. To her this represented a victory of reclaiming God's presence and power in the land, to prayerfully believe for God's promise of the "one new man" in Ephesians 2:14-15. It is noteworthy to mention the order in which they all went through the tunnel. Sherri recognized that the men, the soldiers, were last.

Operation Olive Branch

In her heart, she wanted them to be first, representing the answer to her prayers that the men in the church would lead the way.

Years later, I would go through that same tunnel. This time my friend, Billy Morgan, who is a part of *East River Ministries*, was in front of me, leading the way. He had taken the courageous step to go through this tunnel, and encouraged me to do so to, to reconnect with something Sherri had done, and complete something spiritually. This time, a man, Billy, was symbolically in front, walking through this dark tunnel by faith. Billy even pointed out at the time that this is how *East River* would be, walking by faith, and the men leading the way.

Aliyah is the mysterious word, which means *to go up*. We have been talking primarily about people making spiritual aliyah, coming up higher in our vision for Israel. Now we will focus for a moment on the physical aliyah, which is immigration to Israel for the Jewish people. Sherri had mentioned a woman named Deborah Kellogg many times. About six months after Sherri died, I was going through some papers, when I came across Deborah's name and phone number. I called her. She had not heard about Sherri's family being in the plane crash. She was stunned to hear this news, as we all had been.

After a lengthy conversation with Deborah, she invited me to come to a conference she was having on St. Simon's Island at Epworth by the Sea, in Sherri's place, since she would have gone. (I had been there before as I tell about in, "The Mystery of the Open Doors.") It is a United Methodist campground, and Sherri and I had been there when we were digging into our Methodist roots.

This was my first solo car trip, driving myself six hours to Georgia to go to this conference. This was a big step for me just to drive there by myself because I really had not gone anywhere much in my adult life. God was getting me out of my box.

The reason this was significant is because it connected me with Deborah. She and her husband are the founders and directors of a ministry called *The Cyrus Foundation*. This organization is about praying for and helping with the return of the Jewish people to

Israel. *The Cyrus Foundation* actually helps get the people and their belongings to Israel. *East River Ministries* has now had several projects to raise money, through *The Cyrus Foundation*, to help Jewish families fulfill their dream and fulfill Bible prophecy.

Aliyah is one of the most important concepts in the Bible. The reason is because it underlines the fact that God's people are returning to their land. This refutes the replacement theology mentality of the times we live in, where the church in many cases feels like they have replaced Israel, but the Bible clearly shows that when God makes a covenant promise, that He does not break it. He promised Israel that the land would be theirs forever and ever and He promised that they would return.

My prayer is, "Lord, let me help them to return, by sharing these stories with whoever will listen. May I never be a hindrance to the Jewish people being able to fulfill their divine destiny." I believe it is the church's responsibility to pray for them to return, and also to pray for their salvation by believing in their Jewish Messiah, Jesus. This will happen as we continue to pray and bless.

The Secret of the Blue M&M's

A while back, I was introduced to the idea of personalized colored M&M's. I found out that you can order them in custom colors with custom words on them. As I was beginning to celebrate Israel's 60th anniversary, I thought, "What can I do with Blue and White M&M's, since Israel's national colors are blue and white?" I was thinking they might be a good tool for making my church aware of the celebration. I had it in my mind to order them, but hadn't done it yet.

I went to visit Alice during this time, who was my ninety-one year old Jewish friend in a local nursing home. I had been visiting her for about eight years. (For the complete story of my friend Alice, please read the next chapter, "The Search for the Lost Coin.") As we sat there chatting, I looked over at her bedside table. I was shocked when I saw a big blue stuffed M&M! What are the odds? I mean, it could have even been any color; it was blue and white!

It was the 4th of July, which also just so happened to be Alice's birthday. I remembered the blue and white M&M's I had just been thinking of that had to do with the birthday of the nation of Israel. Now, here I was with this little Jewish lady, staring at this big blue M&M, on her birthday and also on the birthday of the United States of America. Anyone who knows me knows that I feel strongly that the United States and Israel go together. It was pointed out to me once that there is a USA right in the middle of JerUSAlem. This is a constant reminder to us that we as a country need to stand with Israel.

As I went home and thought about what God was saying, and what He would have me do, an idea began to form. I knew that Alice didn't have much money, and sometimes East River would help Alice out by blessing her with some funds. We hadn't done this in a while, so I decided to use this blue and white M&M to do something for her as well as myself since the blue and white M&M was significant to me at that time. I knew she liked to go to the vending machines, and that was one of the things she would look forward to if she had money.

I felt the Lord leading me to give her sixty dollars for the 60th anniversary of Israel. Also, a few days before, I had opened a big bag of M&M's, and had already pulled out all the blue M&M's for my Israel's 60th project. I now meticulously counted out sixty of them, bagged them up, and put them with the sixty dollars, along with a little Israel flag.

The Jewish Shabbat eve came, the Sabbath, which was a Friday night. My idea was to buy Alice's big blue M&M for sixty dollars. I took some Challah, which is braided egg bread, and grape juice, and went into her room. I told her we were going to celebrate Shabbat. This brought back a memory for her from long ago of her Bubbe, or grandmother, making this special bread every week. As she munched on her bread, I explained to her that she had something I needed to buy.

"What?" she said.

"Your stuffed blue M&M."

"You're crazy!" she laughed. "Honey, I'll just give it to you."

"No, Alice, I need to buy it for sixty dollars," I said.

She couldn't believe it, but she gladly sold it to me.

When I got home, I sat the stuffed blue M&M on my bedside table. The next morning, I realized for the first time that the M&M had a "thumbs up" on its white-gloved hand. It almost seemed like the Lord was giving me His affirmation or approval. I smiled at the thought.

The next morning, I was reading in the Word and was reminded of the truth that it's not by my works, but by what He has already accomplished on the cross that I am affirmed and approved of by the Lord. Now, the "thumbs up" on the M&M seemed to be reminding me that God approves of all of us, Jew and Gentile, because of Jesus and His death on the cross.

I read the entire book of Hebrews that day. It was life-changing and radical. I read it in a different way than ever before. He is the Great High Priest who has perfectly fulfilled the commandments of God for me. I knew that any real healing or deliverance that any of us can realize in this world will only be because we receive His already finished work. It's that simple.

That afternoon, I felt the Lord using the blue M&M and its thumbs up to say to me, "I want to be first in your life. I love you and want to be with you as your first priority every day for the rest of your life, and you can love doing what I have called you to do!" Now, I felt that the "thumbs up" meant from the Lord, "You are free to follow me, and I am taking you into the places that your heart desires, because these are actually my desires for you, but first you must have your priorities right. Do you understand?" "Yes, Lord, I understand." A month before, He had asked me, like Peter, "Do you love me? Feed my sheep."

Speak to me, Lord, through whatever creative ways you want to, even blue M&M's, and lead me wherever you want me to go, always thinking about your chosen people, Israel.

The Search for the Lost Coin

One time I went with our Music Minister and other members from church to play and sing hymns at a local nursing facility. I was playing my violin along with the singers, and we had finished playing through our song list and were about to leave. Some of the elderly people had been singing along, and others were just sitting there in their wheelchairs, in their own little worlds. As we had played, I was thinking about how most of these elderly people had probably known the Lord throughout their long lives. I realized that they had seen hardships and sufferings, but by the light in their eyes, as we sang and played, I could see that they had hope. Their hope was that they would soon cross over to the other side and meet Jesus.

As I played, my mind wandered to where it does many times. I began thinking about how, according to Romans 1:16, the gospel of Jesus is for the Jew first. It made me sad to think about the many elderly Jewish people who would have to cross over, not having known Him as their Lord and Messiah. I do not know why God particularly burdened my heart concerning the Jewish people, but I have to believe that most Bible-believing Christians have that same burden inside them somewhere, even if it has not come to full visibility yet.

When we were finished, I was talking to one of the workers at the center who happened to be a friend of mine. What I said next, I had not planned to say, but as it has happened many times, God's grace took control of me. When that happens, He does for me what I cannot do for myself. I found myself saying to my friend,

"Are there any Jewish people that live here?" It was a pretty casual and off-handed question. But her answer, literally, changed my life. She said,

"Actually, there is one Jewish lady here. Her name is Alice. Would you like to meet her?"

"Yes!" I said.

She took me straight to Alice's room. She was sitting in a wheelchair, bent over with arthritis. My friend said,

"Alice, there is someone here who wants to meet you!" Alice looked up, straight at me, and the first thing out of her mouth was,

"Is that a Star of David you are wearing?" I was indeed wearing my necklace with the Star of David, the one with the cross in the center.

"Yes, it is." I said. She then asked the second question.

"Are you Jewish?" My answer to her, literally, changed *her* life forever.

"No, I'm not," I said, "but..." Then I sat down with her, and spent the next two hours telling her about her Jewish Messiah.

She was intensely interested, asking me questions and giving me her thoughts and doubts throughout our time together. She would make statements like, "I just never understood the idea of the virgin birth." I honestly don't remember now every way I explained it all to her, but I do know that the Lord was with me and gave me exactly the words to say that she apparently needed to hear.

At the end of our time together, I almost asked her, "Alice, would you like to think about all we've talked about, and I will come back at another time and we can talk more?" Without notice or warning, the Holy Spirit changed the words that came out of my mouth, and instead, I found myself asking, "Alice, do you understand all that I have explained, and are you ready to pray and receive Yeshua/Jesus as your Jewish Messiah?"

I realized that none of us are promised tomorrow, and she was already in her eighties. I was surprised, and yet, delighted, that her answer to me was, "What have I got to lose?" She said it with a shrug of her shoulders, and yet with real sincerity. It was just said with her strong New York City accent and mannerisms. She humbly bowed her head, as we prayed the prayer, and she repeated after me her repentance of sin, and her acceptance of Jesus' perfect atonement for her sin on the cross. She was saved and on her way to heaven. She never looked back. From that time forward, she continually told anyone and everyone who came across her path, "I am a newly-born again Christian Jew."

I was as blown away as Alice was with the circumstances surrounding that day. From her perspective, she was just sitting in her room, alone, with no hope and no joy. Suddenly, in a short period of time, her whole life was changed, because God Himself had searched her out, and I knew this was the case. There was grace all over this whole encounter!

I had nothing in me that would have naturally searched Alice out. As I mentioned before, I had not planned to say what I said when I asked if there was a Jewish person at the nursing home that day. And yet, within a few minutes, there I was in the room, sharing the love of Jesus with this precious Jewish woman. I told her that Jesus had searched her out, and He had found her. She was truly amazed that He could love her that much, and I was truly amazed and blessed that He would use me in that way. It was one of the greatest joys and blessings of my entire life, to lead one of His own, one of the chosen people, to a relationship with Him.

In the parable of the lost coin in Luke 15:1-7, I could truly relate to how God must have felt that day, and how the angels rejoiced! It says, beginning in vs. 4,

What man among you, if he has a hundred sheep and has lost one of them, does not leave the ninety-nine in the open pasture, and go after the one which is lost, until he finds it? And when he has found it, he lays it on his shoulders, rejoicing. And when he comes home, he calls together his friends and his neighbors, saying to them, 'Rejoice with me, for I have found my sheep which was lost! I tell you that in the same way, there will be more joy in heaven over one sinner who repents, than over ninety-nine righteous persons who need no repentance (vv. 4-7).

Alice and I spent the next several years together, discussing Jesus, her family, and her struggles. Since she had not been raised in an extremely observant Jewish home, many times, as I was learning about my own Jewish roots of my Christian faith, I would share things with her about hers. I would teach her things concerning the Jewish feasts - Passover, Purim, Tabernacles, and we discussed how Jesus was seen in each of them…how He was the fulfillment of them.

I would sometimes take my violin and play for her. Some of those times, I would play Jewish sounding music, and other times, I would play hymns. She always had a request when I played. She always asked me to play, "In the Garden," a Christian hymn. My guess was that she had heard it sung in the nursing home by the Christian residents, and now that their faith was hers as well, she had a special love for the song.

On every single visit I ever made to her, she told me about her only daughter, Sally, who had died of cancer. This one event had shaped her life more than any other. She had gone through the suffering and death of her only beloved and begotten child, a daughter. Perhaps this was the reason why it was so easy for her to accept the idea that God loved her so much that He could actually give His only beloved and begotten Son to die for her. As much as it hurts for any of us to lose someone we love, the idea that God the Father gave His Son to die so that we could live forever with Him is a truth that is hard to grasp but incredibly wonderful at the same time.

After Alice accepted Jesus, she always had the hope that she would meet Sally one day, and I have hope for that too, because at some point in our conversations, she had told me that Sally had joined the Methodist church and had raised her family in church. My hope is not in the denomination or the church that Sally attended, but in the hope that because she had chosen to go to church, there was an indication that she had enjoyed a genuine personal relationship with Jesus. My hope was that she had simply put her faith in Jesus, the Messiah. If so, I knew that Alice would indeed see her daughter again someday.

One time, early on in our relationship, I had felt inspired to make Alice a little silk banner for her door. She had always loved the symbolism of the Star of David with the cross in it. I had given her two necklaces with that particular symbol, but most jewelry I had given her had mysteriously disappeared. A homemade banner, I thought, might be different. I hoped that maybe it would stick around a while, and my hunch turned out to be right. That banner hung on her door for the rest of her life. It had the symbol of the "Messianic Seal" on it, which was a menorah, a Christian fish and a Star of David in the center. This was a constant reminder to Alice of her newfound Christian/Jewish faith. She did not have to give up her Jewish identity to become a Christian. Jesus was Himself Jewish, after all.

This symbol and the fact that she was openly Jewish and Christian did not come without its share of spiritual warfare for Alice, even within her own living environment in the nursing home. She told me several times of how her roommate, who happened to be a Baptist, had called her a "blankety-blank Jew." This had apparently hurt Alice deeply, because she replayed it to me over and over. This, however, gave Alice a chance to practice unconditional love and forgiveness.

I also witnessed Alice make use of her time in the nursing home, by praying for others who were hurting. She mostly did this in silent prayers, but when she heard someone crying out down the hall, or knew a roommate was going through a challenge, she would lay awake at night, praying for them. This gave her a reason for living. It gave her life meaning and purpose, to think of others, rather than her own suffering. Alice had indeed suffered throughout her long life. Not only had she lost her daughter to cancer, but she'd had a couple of aneurysms and strokes that had caused her to have to endure terrible surgeries, and had left her paralyzed on the right side.

The only family she had left was her grandson and his wife and their children. They had initially tried to care for Alice in their home, but the grandson's wife had cancer herself. Finally, she was no longer able to care for her. They then placed Alice in the nursing home, visiting and bringing her home for visits as often as possible. Many, many times, Alice asked me to pray for this granddaughter-in-law, for healing. We had done so, and the reports that kept coming back were always good. Alice had continual hope that God was answering her prayers.

I had never actually met Alice's family, because our paths had never crossed during visits; however, one day, I felt inspired to leave a letter for them, requesting that if anything ever happened to Alice, to please call me. One day, the call came. I was told that they had brought Alice home. Their children had grown up and moved out, and they had a vacant room, and wanted to try to give her a home environment. Just as she got to their home, though, she began to let go. She had gone downhill quickly, and when the family realized she was not getting better, they had called Hospice, who was helping them to make her comfortable for her "transition." It was at this point, that I made my final visit to Alice.

I came to the realization that day, that I was probably one of her only friends. As I cried together with this couple who was her only family, we were able to release her to the Lord. I asked about a funeral, and they had decided that there wouldn't be one, because Alice hadn't wanted it. We tried to wake her up that day, and I spoke to her over and over that I was there. She had waited patiently so many times, in between my visits, and each time I had visited her over the years, her first words were always, "How ya doin', Sweethaaat, long time no see!" She was always so happy to see me, even though I knew I had stayed away too long in between my visits. She always loved me unconditionally and she always received my friendship and love, as I did hers.

This visit, however, was different. She didn't wake up, and she didn't say, "How ya doin', Sweethaaat…" I leaned forward, kissing her forehead, and praying gently over her. Tears began to flow, as I thought about the blessing and privilege that the Lord had given me to know Alice. No one could ever know the joy she had brought into my life, knowing that we shared faith in the Jewish Messiah. She was truly one of the biggest blessings of my entire life.

As I prayed and cried, Hebrew words began to form in my prayers. These were words of blessing in Hebrew that I had learned over the years. This was what so many of us in the Protestant denominations have heard prayed in English, at the closing of services – the "Benediction." In actuality, it was Aaron, the High Priest's prayer over the children of Israel from Numbers 6:22-27, which says,

> *Then the Lord spoke to Moses, saying, "Speak to Aaron and to his sons, saying, 'Thus you shall bless the sons of Israel. You shall say to them: 'The Lord bless you and keep you, the Lord make His face shine upon you, and be gracious unto you, the Lord lift up His countenance upon you and give you peace – Shalom.' In this way you are to put my name on the people of Israel, so that I will bless them.'"*

It seemed so appropriate now – a benediction, of sorts, or a final blessing over Alice.

1 Peter 2:9 says that He has made us to be *"a chosen race, a royal priesthood, a holy nation, a people for God's own possession."* I truly felt like a priest as I prayed these words in Hebrew over Alice:

Y'varekh'kha Adonai v'yishmerekha,
Ya'er Adonai panav eleikha vichunekka,
Yissa Adonai panav eleikha v'yasem l'kha shalom.

As I prepared to leave, I asked her family if we could gather around her bed and hold hands and pray. I began praying with my hand on her head, and releasing her to the Lord, into the arms of her Messiah. We all cried together, and I prayed for the family, and for her. On my drive home, I realized that I had indeed acted in the role of "officiating minister" at probably the only "memorial service" she would ever have. I thought how sweet of God to not only give me the honor and blessing of helping my friend be birthed into the Kingdom years before, but also being there to usher her "home". On both occasions, it felt a little like I was a midwife, helping in a birth, into new and eternal life.

My life would not have been the same without this rich experience that began many years ago. To lead one of His precious chosen people to Him is something that can never be replaced. It was so incredibly meaningful, and it was all Him. Jesus was the initiator, the One who went seeking for the "lost coin," and she was found. I just got to be the feet that brought the beautiful good news to her. Now I know how those angels in heaven feel when they are rejoicing over one sinner who repents and turns to Jesus.

The Message of the Open Doors

Sherri stood in the driveway of my home in Panama City. As we looked at the front bumper tag that she had just had airbrushed, I knew that I was a part of her. The tag had a picture of the Messianic Seal, or the One New Man symbol, as some are calling it in modern terminology. This had a Jewish menorah at the top, a Christian fish at the bottom and a Star of David in the center.

She'd had some words written onto the tag, something along the lines of, "Call Forth the Message of the Messianic Seal." She felt that as she was driving all over the country, that she was prophetically proclaiming that the Jews and the Gentiles were becoming one in the Messiah. She was eccentric, but I loved her.

The "Messianic Seal" was something that was discovered on some pieces of pottery that dated back to the time of the early church. About forty pieces of this pottery were found in the area of the upper room that is mentioned in the book of Acts. A monk discovered it in the 1960's, after it had been hidden for about two-thousand years. This symbol not only reinforces the Jewishness of our Christian faith, since all in the early church were Jewish believers, but it also emphasizes the coming together of the Jew and the Gentile as One New Man in the Messiah as spoken of in Ephesians 2:14-15.

Sherri had a zeal and passion for the things God had called her to do. I also had a love and passion for the Jewish people and Israel. Her passion was on a different level than mine, in that it got her out beyond the sphere of everyday life and into a great unknown adventure. It was at this point in our lives that God began to really put us together for a divine mission.

I had been studying, not only my Jewish roots, but also my Methodist roots. I had been a member of the Methodist church for many years, and there were many Methodists in my family. As I searched back in history, however, I discovered the fervent founder of the Methodist church, John Wesley. His faith inspired me. He was always outside the walls of the church, preaching the gospel in the open air to anyone who would come. He was one of the catalysts for the First Great Awakening which took place in the 1700's in England.

Sherri was a student at the United Methodist Seminary at Asbury in Orlando, Florida. She was studying and reading some of the same things there that I was studying and reading on my own. I was a mom and housewife, homeschooling my kids and studying the Bible, Jewish roots, and Methodist history on my own, and she was in school, studying, and putting feet to her faith.

Somewhere along the way, she got it into her head that she would need to go to Savannah, GA, where John and Charles Wesley, the founders of Methodism first came to America. She wanted to do a prayer initiative there, going all the way back to the roots. The reason for this is because she had discovered that the modern-day United Methodist Church seemed to have turned their backs on Israel, and were calling for the USA and the church to remove support for the nation, financially and other ways. That was all I really knew about the situation, as I had not yet discovered the United Methodist Church's resolution number 312, "Opposition to Israeli Settlements in Palestinian Land," and wouldn't until after Sherri had already gone to heaven.

That day standing in my driveway, looking at her car tag and discussing the fact that she was going to take this trip, she encouraged me to go with her. I didn't think I would, but God had other plans for me. I did wind up going, and that trip changed my life.

Driving down the highway, with the praise music blasting, we were on an adventure! When we got to Jacksonville, we picked up two other intercessors whom Sherri knew, but I didn't. We went on toward Savannah and it was late by the time we got there. I remember us driving around Savannah late at night, exhausted, and looking for a hotel. We finally found one in a part of town that seemed a bit lonely and isolated. We went in and slept. Here we were, in Savannah, GA, oddly enough, on a mission to pray for the Jewish people, and also for the United Methodist Church.

The first of the confirmations happened the next morning as I opened the hotel room door. I couldn't believe what I saw. Directly across from our hotel room was a Jewish synagogue! It had a Magen David, or Star of David, on it and something very unusual. On the side of the brick wall was an art depiction that it took us a minute to figure out. It was made out of huge black chains. We thought, "Why are there huge black chains as art on the outside of this building?" We were never completely sure, but it spoke to us of the bondage to slavery that the Israelites were under at times throughout history. It also reminded us that we are all still in bondage to a type of slavery as we live in a world of sin. Yeshua, the Jewish Messiah, died to set us free. We used the building as a prayer point. We all faced the building, extended our hands toward it, and prayed for freedom to come to these precious Jewish people.

Later, we went into downtown Savannah and met with a lady there who had done a lot of praying all over the city. She lived there, and was very familiar with it, and knew other prayer warriors. We told her of our mission there and what we felt we had to do in praying for the Methodist church.

We went around to various locations, praying, including the old Christ Episcopal Church, where John Wesley was first affiliated, since he was Anglican at the time he was in America. We then went over to the First United Methodist Church to pray. We had heard a story that at some point in history, the Jewish synagogue had burnt down, and the Methodists invited the Jewish community to hold their services there. This kindness from history prompted us to pray that the Methodist church today would continue to have the same love and honor for the Jewish people.

Another place we went was the Jewish synagogue, one of the oldest in the nation. It was this same Jewish community that dated back to the time of Oglethorpe that John and Charles Wesley had lived among during their stay here. We had read in a particular history book that John Wesley had become "acquainted with the Jews of Savannah." He studied Spanish in order to converse with them and, says his diary, some of them "seem nearer the mind that was in Christ than many of those who called Him Lord."[3]

As we were leaving this synagogue, we picked up one of their brochures from the table and I laid it on the floor of the van, not looking at it too closely. I noticed that it was folded in such a way that it looked like a door opening. This small action would later become another clue that we were moving with the Holy Spirit in our prayers.

The reason we had decided to make this journey to begin with was because we had heard of John Wesley's love for the Jewish people. We wanted to call forth those righteous roots of Methodism and believe for a re-kindling of love for God's chosen people by the people called Methodists.

We went to Tybee Island to pray in the location where John and Charles first touched land in America. As we stood there praying, I'm sure we looked a little comical. There were a group of us there, praying hard, with our hands extended toward the water (toward Jerusalem), and we had a Jerusalem flag, an Israeli flag, a couple of shofar's (ram's horns), some of us were wearing Jewish prayer shawls, and we were worshiping with flags. Someone had brought a boom box with worship music.

To be honest, I felt really uncomfortable with the whole thing, but I went along with it, because I knew it was the right thing for us to be doing. God had guided our steps and confirmed them, and I was not to question how it came about. However, when a group of about two hundred school children and their teachers came out to the beach for a field trip, I found myself praying that we would be invisible to them. As it turned out, they didn't seem to notice us at all. If they did, they may have thought we were

---

3   Rufus Learsi, *The Jews in America – A History*, Ktav, 1954.

rehearsing for a play or something. I'm a little ashamed of myself for how I felt that day, considering the magnitude of what we were doing as far as God's purposes were concerned.

We then moved on to St. Simon's Island. By this time, during our prayers that we had prayed all over the place, there was a common theme that had continued to come up. We found ourselves praying for open doors within the United Methodist church as it related to Israel. We weren't sure what that meant, but we went with it and continued on our journey.

When we got to St. Simon's, we went to Epworth by the Sea, which is a United Methodist campground, rich in Methodist history. The location had a beautiful little chapel with lovely stained glass depictions of the Wesley brothers. Charles Wesley, in particular, had stayed on St. Simon's Island during his time in America. He later went on to write over six thousand hymns for "the people called Methodists," which are now sung by many denominations all over the world.

As we were praying around the grounds, I walked over to the chapel door to see if we could go inside. It had a sign outside that said, "Service in Progress"; however, I didn't hear anything going on inside, so I tried to open the door. I could not. It would not open at all. I was persistent and pulled a little harder, but it still would not budge.

I left that area and continued to walk around the grounds. I began thinking about Charles Wesley and all those beautiful hymns he had written, and was thinking how wonderful it would be to see those songs sung in a modern way within our churches, with a bit of a contemporary flair to them! That day, I was praying that God would do just that, so that we didn't lose the beauty and meaning behind the words to the hymns, but it would draw younger people because of the sound.

That actually isn't much different of a concept than what Charles did in his day when he took the modern bar tunes that were popular for that time period, and added his words to them to draw the masses of people who were coming into the church.

As I prayed this prayer, as if in response to what I was praying, suddenly, a huge church bell that was on the grounds began to chime out the music to, "O For A Thousand Tongues," one of Charles' hymns! It was a powerful moment for me, helping me to feel that God was right there with us, and was indeed hearing our prayers.

After a while, we decided to try again to go into the chapel. We had never moved from the grounds, and yet we had not seen

anyone come out of the building. This time, however, when we tried the door it opened wide, so we entered.

We had a powerful prayer time in that little chapel, just the four of us who had continued on to St. Simon's. We prayed for the Methodist Church to stand with Israel. Suddenly, as we were praying, we heard some sort of loud noise outside. We thought people were coming and wanting to get into the church, so we finished up our prayer, and went to the door. Once again, the door would not open! We were locked inside the building! Perhaps it was just the fact that it was eighteenth-century doorknobs, but still, it was interesting how it all played out.

It was almost humorous, but also a little scary. We all tried, and literally shook the door, and it would not open for us at all. We felt like there must be some spiritual warfare going on, so we prayed some more! After a while, we tried the door again, and it opened right up!

We felt this was quiet prophetic utterance of the word we had been given for open doors within the Methodist church concerning Israel. We stood in the doorway of the little Lovely Lane Chapel and prayed once more for the doors to be open!

Now we were finished with our assignment, and were ready to leave. As we got into the van, I looked down on the floor and saw the brochure from the Jewish synagogue. I noticed once again that there were doors on the front. I opened them up. Inside was a message about them inviting visitors in, and that their "doors were always open." We laughed at the goodness of God to give us confirmations along the way.

I will finish this story by saying, incidentally, that two months after we got home from our trip, I was watching TV one day, and I saw the brand new commercial put out by the United Methodist Church. They were promoting the church as having, "Open Hearts, Open Minds, and Open Doors." It doesn't get much better than that! I pray now that the Methodist church will actually apply this to our understanding about where we need to stand with Israel. We need to open our hearts, open our minds and open our doors of understanding that we cannot turn our backs on God's chosen people. It extends all the way back to our roots.

Hannah's Hanukkah Adventure

Who would have ever thought that the mall would be the place where you could share the love of Yeshua with Israel? Thank God for the creative genius of Kiosks! All kinds of things are sold in Kiosks, those little booths in the center of the mall. Israeli young people come every year to earn money by selling Dead Sea products and various other items in some of these booths. For the Christian lover of Israel, it is the perfect opportunity to make God's love known to those who have come from across the ocean.

Israel is always on the verge of war, or at war. One time, Israel was striking Gaza because of continual rocket launches into Israel. These rocket launches had been going on since Gaza was given over to the Palestinian Arabs in 2005. Many of these young people who come here from Israel know someone in the military that is in harm's way.

It seems to me that when the Holy Spirit is in something, that things just click. That is what happened on the day when the realization came to me that it was the last night of Hanukkah, and at the mall were some young people who were away from their families. I prayed as I drove down the road, "Lord, put your thoughts in my mind. What do you want me to do to bless them?"

East River Ministries is a ministry based at my church that loves and blesses Israel. I had a small amount of *East River* funds to work with, so as I was praying about it and pondering this question, the first thought came:

"Starbucks Gift Cards."

"OK, sounds good. Is there more?" I wondered.

"Stop at Hallmark." The prompting from the Lord seemed clear.

"OK." I thought, as I turned in. I walked around like I knew what I was looking for. I never make decisions this quick, but as soon as I spotted the magnetic bookmarks with the dove and olive branch I knew that I had found it.

"It has a New Testament scripture," I thought to myself.

"It's OK. Let them know that a Christian is loving and blessing them. You won't offend them. They will just like to know you love them." Was I done? I didn't think so.

"Stop at CVS."

I found Lindor Truffles, wrapped in blue paper.

After I had everything I needed, I taped the items together along with an *East River Ministries* card. Then off to the mall I went.

As I approached the first group of Jewish girls, I explained that I am a Christian who loves Israel, and wanted to wish them a Happy Hanukkah. I told them about *East River*, and how we love and bless them, and pray for them, especially with the war that was going on at the time. I did this at three different Kiosks. I loved their Hebrew-sounding names. I asked them all about their name meanings. They hugged and kissed me, and thanked me, and admired a necklace I was wearing that was from Israel. It had a key with the Hebrew writing on it. We discussed the meaning of the Hebrew words on the necklace. It was good conversation. After we finished talking, I let them know that *East River Ministries* was there for them, and to call if they needed prayer or anything.

One interesting thing that happened was that the girls called one of the other guys over to take our picture. He was not Jewish, but had an accent that made me suspect he was from the Middle East. As we were standing there, and I was telling the girls that I hoped so much that our government would not put pressure on Israel to give up more land or divide Jerusalem, the young man had an interesting comment.

"It will never happen," he said.

"How do you know?" I asked.

"It's in the Bible," he replied. "You bless Israel, you are blessed, you curse Israel, you are cursed. Simple."

"You're not Jewish, are you?" I asked.

"I am Palestinian Christian, and my family is Palestinian Christian," he replied. I realized that having Yeshua in your heart opens our understanding, no matter what your ethnic background.

I am so thankful to the Holy Spirit for the timing and the opportunity to find everything needed to bless these Israelis. These young people from Israel are in many malls in America and they are far away from their homeland. It's a great opportunity to form relationships and to bless God's chosen people.

The Clue in the Old Library

I must tell you now, how the name *East River Ministries* came into being. This is the name of the ministry God has given me, which is to do a couple of things:

A. Be a blessing to Israel in a tangible way, and pray for their restoration, both physically, emotionally and spiritually.

B. Help the modern-day church to understand why it is important to stand with Israel and the Jewish people.

This came from a scripture which was my initial call into ministry, Isaiah 49:6, which says,

Is it too small a thing that you should be my servant, to raise up the tribes of Jacob, and to restore the preserved ones of Israel. I will also make you a light of the nations...

(This entire story is told in "The Mystery of the Star Sapphire Ring" chapter.)

Although this was a scripture about Jesus, it was also given to Paul, and since I am in Christ, I received it as a word for myself when it seemed to lift off the page to me as I was reading and praying many years ago. I also believe it applies to any believer in Christ who will receive this word for themselves.

Ezekiel 47 tells the story of the River of Life in the restored Jerusalem. Verse 1 reads:

Then he brought me back to the door of the house, and behold, water was flowing from under the threshold of the house toward the east for the house faced east. And the water as flowing down from under, from the right side of the house, from south of the altar.

This verse really became significant to me as I was serving at Springfield United Methodist Church in Panama City, Florida. I had been making a large banner for the church, based on this scripture. The banner depicted the River of God, and the laver of bronze from the temple in Jerusalem. At the top of the banner, I was trying to depict Ezekiel's temple, and was in the process of praying about how best to do this, when I had a realization. Coincidentally (or not), our church faced east, the same as in Ezekiel's temple.

When I realized this, I decided to make the temple at the top of the banner with the river flowing out of the south side toward the East. I depicted it to look a little like our church, although not exactly. In my mind, I saw our church as sort of a spiritual temple of God, with the River of Life, the Holy Spirit, flowing through us. As it says in Ezekiel 47:9,

...every living creature which swarms in every place where the river goes, will live.

This also applies to us personally, as the river of life flows from our innermost being, going out into the world to bring His message of love and peace and redemption.

Later, after my friend Sherri's death, I felt that *East River Ministries* would be an appropriate name. This is because of another clue that the Lord put in my path as the ministry was in formation. I was in the process of praying about what the name of the ministry was to be. I was in the library at the United Methodist Church where I worked. I was on a break and just browsing through the books on the shelf. Suddenly, a book grabbed my attention, as if it were the only book there. The spine of the book said, *East River* and there was a picture of a Jewish menorah (lampstand) with a cross dangling from a chain, and a white dove over the top of the menorah. It was a book by Sholem Asch, a Jewish writer. Naturally, based on all that had happened concerning my understanding of Ezekiel 47 when I was making that banner, I was drawn to take the book off the shelf.

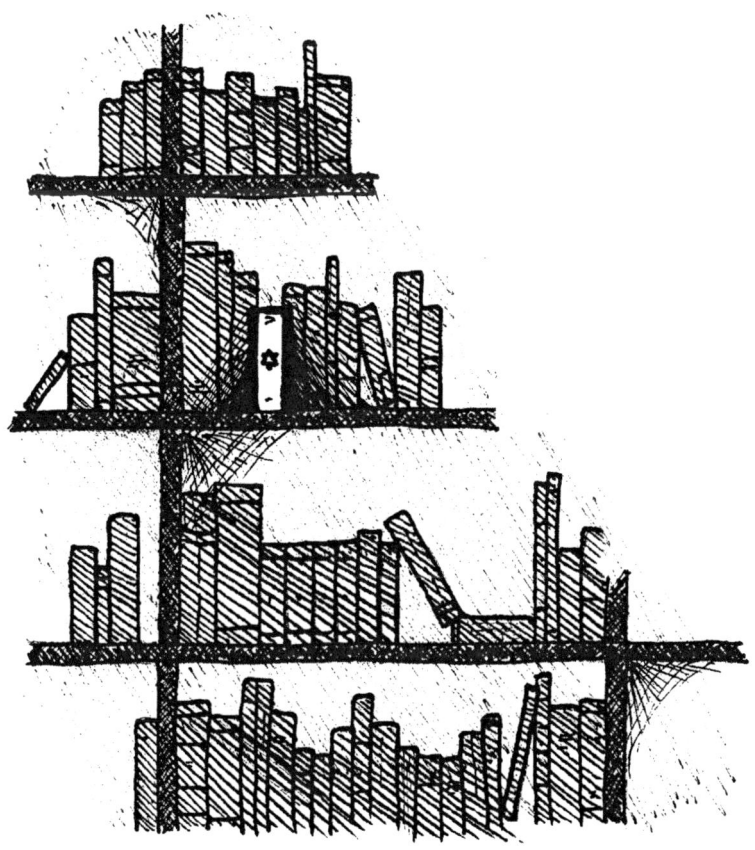

What I saw on the front cover was even more compelling. It was a picture of a Jewish man with a Star of David over his shoulder, and a Christian woman holding a Bible with a cross on the front, and they were standing together. In the background was a scene of a dock at the turn of the century in New York City. Glancing at the first chapter, immediately, I came to understand that there was an actual East River in New York City. I suppose there is a first time to learn everything!

Anyway, it was in this moment I knew God had dropped another clue, or connected another dot along my path. I knew this was to be the name of the ministry that I was to carry out as a major part of my life's purpose. *East River Ministries* became the official name, all within a few minutes. The picture on the front cover of the book showed a good visual of the "one new man" of Ephesians 2:15, which is Jew and Gentile, one in the Messiah. For clarification purposes, Gentile refers to any nation that is not Jewish. This is sometimes also referred to in scripture as "Greek," as in Romans 1:16 which reads:

For I am not ashamed of the gospel of Christ (Messiah), for it is the power of God unto salvation to everyone who believes, to the Jew first, and also to the Greek (or Gentiles, or Nations). (my paraphrase)

I normally don't read fiction books, (OK, except maybe for Nancy Drew) but this one held great interest for me. I learned much about the melting pot of the United States, coming together along the waterfront of the East River. There were even more clues as I read the book. One thing in particular stands out in my memory. The book was describing how all the people in the neighborhood along the East River, from different nationalities, came together with a common garden plot in someone's back yard. Each person, whether Jews, Irish, Italians, Germans, etc., would plant things that were native to the homeland from which they had come. The garden was described as having the "fruits of the nations" within it.[4]

This, too, was meaningful to me, as the Lord had already spoken to me many times before, that as we put the "Jew First" (Romans 1:16) in our prayers and in sharing the gospel of Jesus, we would have the fruit of the nations as an inheritance. This means that all the nations of the world will ultimately come to the Messiah Yeshua (Jesus). I felt he was showing me that this is His plan for bringing the world (nations) to Himself. Jesus is the Garden Plot that we all have in common.

This is how *East River Ministries* began in earnest. Not long after, I would find myself in the state of New York on a prayer journey

---

4   Sholem Asch, *East River: A Novel of New York*, 1974.

with some friends, praying over the streams and rivers, and calling God's people back to Him. I came to a deeper understanding as I was researching these streams and rivers in New York, realizing that many of them flowed into the East River. It was imbedded, at that time, even deeper into me that I had some sort of connection, not only to the East River of Ezekiel 47, but also to this literal body of water called East River. At the time, I was not sure what it was, but I was determined to find out. Another mystery needed to be solved. (The continuation of this story can be found in the chapter entitled, "Danger in New York City.")

Being a spiritual sleuth is such an adventure!

The Clue in the Crashing Bookcase

After I had established my *East River Ministries* office in an upstairs room of our church, I spent many hours there organizing and arranging my friend Sherri's personal items (see *The Mysterious Wild-Eyed Woman*). I had written a letter to her family after she died and asked if they would save for me anything that might pertain to the Israel ministry. They sent me six bags full of her things and there was always something new to discover as I found places to put everything. Many days I spent reminiscing, praying, crying, and even mourning over the loss of my friend, but mostly, I was in awe and sometimes overwhelmed at the huge responsibility that now seemed to be in my lap. I was to carry on a mission to the land and people of Israel and I was to help the church understand our role with the Jewish people. At times, I would just sit at the foot of the stairs in my office and sob. I would play beautiful Jewish violin music on my i-Pod and soak in the presence of the Lord. So much was birthed inside of me during this time.

There were some odd things that happened in my office from time to time. I do not believe in ghosts, so don't misunderstand what I am about to tell you, but sometimes something would just fall over, like a shelf. OK, the shelf was old and wobbly, so that could be it, but this happened about three times. Every time it would happen, I would be cleaning up the mess and find something of Sherri's that I had not seen before. I would find a DVD, a book, or a CD with some sort of pertinent message for me at that moment.

Never was there a more profound message than the one I found one day after the bookshelf had fallen over once again. Actually, it was more like a crash. I had learned from the other two crashes, and had moved the bookcase across the room and had wedged it up under an attic slant in the roof. I had checked to make sure it was secure, and had left it and thought no more of it.

My friend Billy, who is part of the *East River Ministries* team, was upstairs in the office alone one day. He was sitting on the couch reading a book from one of the other shelves. As Billy was sitting there quietly reading this book, suddenly, with no obvious cause, the bookshelf across the room crashed to the ground again. It crashed, even though I had it wedged up under the attic slant in the roof!

Initially he felt a little panicked, as so many books, tapes, videos, and CD's all fell into a huge pile in the floor. He somehow felt responsible, but realized he wasn't since he really hadn't done anything. He was across the room, and the book he was reading came from a different bookcase altogether.

He looked at the mess, and thought, "I need to pick that up before Hannah sees it." Suddenly, the Holy Spirit stopped him and he literally felt, for some reason, like he was not supposed to touch it, but just tell me about it.

Sunday morning rolled around and I was getting ready to practice with the praise band. As I was standing there warming up my violin, Billy came by and said, "Oh, I almost forgot to tell you, there is a mess in your office for you to clean up!" And then he laughed a bit. I said, "What?" Then he explained what had happened, and that he felt that he was supposed to leave it just as it was for some reason.

When he said that, I immediately felt like I knew the reason had to be because there was something I needed to find as I was cleaning it up. This had been the case the last two times the bookshelf had crashed, and for that matter, even as I was putting things on the shelves to begin with. I had always found significant things that I needed to see or hear involving the ministry.

I was almost excited about going to clean up the mess! It was that same Sunday afternoon that I went back to the church and up the stairs to my office. I quietly opened the door and stepped inside. There was the mess across the room, just as Billy had left it. I put on some good Jewish-style worship music. This almost felt like a worship experience to me because I always encountered God in this room, and particularly if I knew I was looking for something that He was going to show me.

I sat down on the floor, and began to go through the books, tapes, and everything else that had fallen into this huge pile. I looked over each item, and if it didn't catch my attention, I returned it to the shelf. I continued this process for a while, when suddenly, my eye caught a plain cassette that I had never seen. It was not in a case and had a label that said, "Wed. night Bible study at Sherri's." I can't explain it, but I just knew that was it.

I turned off the worship music, and popped it into the cassette player so I could listen while I finished cleaning. Immediately, I was absorbed in the sounds coming from the cassette. I heard Sherri's voice, sharing Bible passages. I heard others that had been at her house for the Bible study, and they were commenting and reading and discussing. It was good to hear her voice again. I still didn't know why I was listening to this cassette, but I continued.

As I kept cleaning, focusing on my task and somewhat passively listening, I suddenly snapped back into reality when I heard Sherri's voice speaking on the cassette. She always had this breathless way of talking because she lived in such a profound place with God. It was almost like she was gasping for air as she exclaimed her amazement over something He had done. This time she was sharing about how her kitchen cabinets had come crashing to the ground! They had fallen off the wall and the glass and dishes had shattered everywhere.

I suddenly remembered that she had told me that story many times. What I remembered was that it had happened during the time that she had just learned about the Kristallnacht, which means, "Night of Broken Glass," where in Germany and Austria in 1938, the Nazis had raided villages and synagogues and shattered the glass in all the windows in their houses of worship.

As Sherri was learning about this horrible thing that had happened to the Jews, she had this experience of her kitchen cabinets crashing to the floor and the glass being shattered. As she shared her experience on the tape, others who were at this Bible study were beginning to chime in with their own stories of experiences they'd had of things falling or crashing.

Sherri also told of how she had been with Marcia, her Jewish friend in Miami long ago, before she was saved, and they had been driving down the highway together when a huge branch came crashing down and shattered their car window. Someone in the room then asked if she thought this was from the Lord. She said she felt it was, and that He was trying to get her attention.

I was stunned. Just as Sherri had felt that God was getting her attention during these things, He had definitely gotten mine, so the question to ask now was, for what was the Lord trying to get my attention? I started thinking, crashed bookshelf, a huge mess to clean up, Sherri's crashed kitchen cabinet, others talking about things crashing, what could it be?

The clue, I believe, that God wanted me to figure out, was what she had been studying when this happened to her. The Kristallnacht. This was just one of many pogroms (violent mob attacks) that the Jewish people had to endure. There were massacres of whole Jewish communities, organized by the governments who were anti-Jewish. They happened on a large scale in Russia, but also carried into Nazi Germany and Austria.

As I sat there on my office floor, I wondered, could this kind of thing ever happen again, and if it did, would we be prepared to help the Jewish people? What if it happened to the Christians, too? Would we be strong enough in our spirits to do the right thing to protect and defend God's chosen people and to do our part to help fulfill God's purposes for them? All these things were going through my mind as I finished cleaning up.

It was not until days later when I was relating this story to Billy, telling him why the Holy Spirit had indeed told him to leave that mess for me to clean up, that I received a further confirmation. As

I told him the story, his eyes grew wide. He then told me what it was that he was reading that day. Believe it or not, he had been reading about the pogroms, those persecutions of the Jewish people that had happened in history, which is what Kristallnacht was.

All of this was surreal. This whole thing had definitely gotten my attention! I was sitting there, cleaning up the mess from a crashed bookshelf, when I found a random tape that I had never heard before. Then heard Sherri's voice on this same random tape talking about her own experience with a crashed shelf, broken glass, and a mess being all over the place, and I thought about what Sherri used to always say, "What are the chances of *that* happening?"

I pray that we will be prepared, just in case we ever have to stand with God's people. The Jews and the Christians may indeed have to support one another in the days ahead. May these things never happen again. No one thought it would happen then, but it did. History tends to have a way of repeating itself, and God tends to have a way of getting our attention, as he did mine and Sherri's and Billy's, because He loves us so much.

Danger in New York City

East River Ministries had just come into existence, when I came to the realization that there was a literal "East River" in New York City. The Lord seemed to be indicating that for me there was a connection between the two, although I wasn't sure what it was yet. It all became clear on an ordinary day, as I was checking my e-mails, and I received a message advertising a book called, *The Beast on the East River*.[5]

I wondered what in the world this could be referring to, as I opened the link. I soon found out that this book by Nathan Tabor, was referring to "The Beast," as the United Nations, and that this huge building actually sits on the East River in New York City. If you haven't read the chapter entitled, "The Clue in the Old Library," this would be a good opportunity to do so, since it will make what I'm about to share in this chapter even more amazing.

I immediately ordered the book, and began to delve into a realm of international politics, something that had never interested me. I came to understand more and more, as I read this book, things I had not understood, like the possible agenda of a one-world government. These were things I had read about in the Bible, but after reading Tabor's explanations, I realized that they were coming to pass before our eyes. I also realized that what goes on in this building, which sits on eighteen acres of international property on the East River in New York City, could be the catalyst for all that is politically correct, but Biblically wrong in our world.

---

5   Nathan Tabor, *The Beast on the East River*, 2006.

I am not suggesting that some good doesn't come from the United Nations. Social justice is good, in and of itself, but apart from the gospel of Jesus Christ, it falls short of the glory of God, because it is based on human understanding, rather than Divine directive.

About the time that I was researching the United Nations, I received another e-mail stating that the President of Iran, who publicly denies the Holocaust and calls for the destruction of the state of Israel, was allowed to speak at the United Nations. There was an outcry because he had not been stopped from speaking some of these things.

Iran is modern-day Persia. I realized that the enemy of Israel is not really a person, but there is an ancient spirit behind the move to annihilate the nation of Israel. Ancient Israel was taken into captivity by the Persians. If you have ever read the book of Esther, you will know that it is centered around the nation of Persia. Esther was a Jewish orphan in hiding. She had been raised by her older Jewish cousin Mordecai, and was chosen by the Persian prince as his wife, not knowing that she was Jewish. In fact, one of the meanings for Esther is "hidden." She was used by God to save her people from destruction by their enemy, Haman. It is the spirit that was inside of Haman who wanted to destroy the Jewish people in the book of Esther.

It was when the Jewish people were in captivity that the Biblical Daniel was also praying for his people. A heavenly messenger appeared to him and said that he had come immediately when Daniel began praying, but he said he was hindered by the Prince of the kingdom of Persia for twenty-one days. The Archangel Michael came and battled against this spiritual enemy so that the heavenly messenger could get through and Daniel's prayers could be answered. In the New Testament book, Ephesians 6:12, it says,

> *For our struggle is not against flesh and blood, but against the rulers, against the powers, against the world forces of this darkness, against the spiritual forces of wickedness in the heavenly places.*

Operation Olive Branch

This helps us to understand the spiritual warfare principle behind the world rulers and authorities. There are spiritual entities that we battle against in the "heavenly places" that are over nations and kingdoms.

As I was driving down the road not long after receiving the book, *The Beast on the East River*, I looked up and saw a sign on a large truck. There was a picture on it of the world with the latitude and longitude grid marks, which reminded me of the pictures I had seen of the logo for the United Nations. It said, "Riverside, a World of Service." I did not know what this company was about and it probably had nothing to do with the United Nations, but that day, the Lord used it to speak something to me. "Riverside" made me think of *East River Ministries*, and seeing the world and those grid marks, it seemed to me that God may have been suggesting that *East River* would be involved in worldwide service of some sort, even if it was only through prayer.

About that time, I saw something in my spirit. Whether it should be called a vision or an impression, I'm not sure, but I did see a clear picture of myself, blowing my friend Sherri's shofar, with my feet on the banks of the East River, facing the United Nations. The shofar is a Hebrew instrument, a ram's horn, which was used to summon the troops for battle, or to herald a message. From that moment, I felt that I was to go to New York City and do something, even if it was just to blow a shofar.

I began talking with a couple of my friends, and soon, a whole team had formed who wanted to go. There were nine of us altogether. My former pastor, Perry Dalton, was a strong encouragement, since I had never led a team anywhere, wasn't sure what I was doing and had only made one plane reservation in my life! This was a huge growing experience for me! Before long, we were all on our way to New York City to pray for Israel, a concept that would not make sense to most of the world, but this was something given by the revelation of God, that we were to go and do.

We felt led to go in early March of that year, which on the Jewish calendar, was the Feast of Purim. This was the time that Jewish people remember Esther and how she saved her people from destruction by Haman. I literally felt like a modern-day Esther, leading a team to pray against a spirit of Haman, on international soil. I remember taking with me a Jerusalem stone that my friend Dalia had given me. I was not sure what I was to do with it, but I felt I should take it.

As if we needed any confirmation, when we arrived at the brownstone, which was a Christian ministry house where we were staying, we went into the one-hundred- or more year-old parlor. To our amazement and delight, coincidentally, on the wall was a panoramic scene of Jerusalem! This was a very encouraging sign to us that we were on the right track.

Soon, we got another incredible clue. At this particular place we were staying, since it was a ministry house, there was only one bathroom per floor. We were staying on the 4th and 5th floors. After we got settled in our rooms, I went into the community bathroom. Suddenly, I was shocked as I heard the most beautiful man's voice I had ever heard, coming up from below and through the window of the bathroom which apparently opened down into the basement of the building. The echo of this voice coming up through this window was amazing. What was more amazing was what was being sung. I stood there and cried as I listened to the operatic voice singing, "Jerusalem, Jerusalem, hark how the angel's sing, Hosanna, in the highest, Hosanna, to our King."

I couldn't believe what I was hearing. Who was singing this song, and why were they singing about Jerusalem, the Holy City of God, for which we had come all the way from Florida and other places to pray ? This was somewhat of a secret mission. No one here in New York City would have known what we were there to pray about. I thought to myself, "Well, it must be Estill," who was a friend who had come on the trip. I had no idea Estill could sing like that, so I opened the window more, and looked down four stories into the basement, and said, "Estill, is that you?"

I heard a voice answer me, "Uh, no, this is not Estill. I'm the janitor." Well, I was overwhelmed. I hollered back down, "Your voice is so beautiful!" He said, "Thank you." I tried to talk him into coming up and singing for our group later; however, as amazing as his voice was, he was too modest and humble, and the private concert never happened. He really sounded like he could have been a Julliard student. He was that good, but what really made me cry, standing there soaking in God's love, was the fact that he was singing, from the basement, about Jerusalem. This indeed was another clue, and a confirmation.

We celebrated Shabbat that night together in the community room of the mission house where we were staying. We prayed together for unity within our group to fulfill what we had come there to do. We prayed for Israel, and the Jewish people of New York and Israel. We also prayed for the President of Iran to even come to know Jesus as his Lord and Savior. Nothing is impossible with God. I remember that as we were worshiping, a song was playing that was exhorting us to "march on" with the "King of the Universe," giving ourselves to Him to do His bidding.

The next morning, we set out to follow our agenda that I had written up before the trip. On our way to pray at the United Nations, we would stop at a Messianic synagogue.

As we walked down the busy New York City street, there was a wonderful, crisp chill in the air. For a few moments, I forgot the seriousness of the journey we were on and decided to take a few pictures of our group coming up the street. I pulled out my camera and turned around, taking a few steps backwards, so that I could get everyone into the shot as they came toward me. Suddenly, the back of my calf bumped something. About that time, my friends, Iris and Anne, both gasped. Iris reached toward me, and possibly pulled me toward her, but I can't even remember.

The title of this story, "Danger in New York City," refers to what happened when I almost fell into a very deep hole in the sidewalk. What my leg had bumped into, below the knee, was a small iron door that stood open in the street. Apparently this was some sort of sewer. I have always felt that an angel must have been positioned behind me to prevent me from falling backwards into the hole! My friends guided me quickly past it, and said, "Don't even look down." It was so deep that if I had fallen in, I would have probably died.

After that, I was so shaken that I could hardly recover to finish the trip to the United Nations. When I realized how close I had come, I was shaking all over. We kept walking toward the subway. Perry took charge of things at that point. I realized that somewhere in all of the madness of what had just transpired, I had lost my written agenda. This also upset me very badly, because it gave all of our names, and where we were staying in New York. Listed on this agenda, was our plan to do spiritual "warfare" at the United Nations. We knew that it was only prayer, but would someone else know that? All I could think of was what might happen if someone got that paper.

I was literally shaking all over. Flashes were going through my mind of the "what if's." What if I had fallen in that hole? I had come so close to death, trying to do something that seemed like it was God-led and inspired. This was when I realized the seriousness of praying for Israel. There are spiritual forces that are not happy about this. Thankfully, the Lord protected me.

As we moved through the subway, it seemed like a long period of time passed, and I still had not recovered. I continued to have flashes of fear all over me. We finally found our way to the Messianic Synagogue for which we had been looking. This is where the Lord helped me to recover to complete the mission. As we entered into the building, we realized that Purim Services were taking place at that moment. They were celebrating Esther's victory over Haman, in saving the Jewish people from destruction.

There was so much joy in the air that morning as they were dancing around the building, worshiping the King of Kings! We lined up on one of the pews and joined in clapping and singing as they brought the Torah around for everyone to touch and kiss. We really sensed that we were one in the Spirit with this Jewish congregation because of our shared Messiah. On the overhead projector were the words to the song they were singing. The words were something like this:

The enemy Haman tried to kill her, but he was not able to kill Esther. She saved her people from destruction.

When I heard this song, I felt as if God were showing me what had just happened. Although the enemy was not happy about what we were there to do, to pray for Israel and Jerusalem and the Jewish people, he was not able to touch me. God did not permit any harm to come to me. Suddenly, I felt strengthened to complete our assignment. I recovered from the near disaster and felt hope and courage rise up in me.

We continued on to the United Nations. We went through security, and only one item was kept and locked up for security by the guards, my shofar. I was questioned about it, since none of them seemed to know what it was. It was a little difficult to explain why I had an instrument of Jewish worship along with me for my tour. Maybe they thought it was a souvenir I had picked up or something. In any case, they held it for me until we were finished with the tour.

We prayed silently as we walked through, looking at everything, each of us praying whatever the Lord put on our hearts to pray for Israel. As we went through the tour of the building, our tour guide took us into the General Assembly hall. We saw where the delegates from all over the world sat and made decisions that had far-reaching effects. The tour guide told us that it takes nine to pass a vote. Suddenly we realized that there were nine of us! We felt that the nine of us were passing votes in the heavenly places through our prayers!

As it was time to leave, I wanted to place my Jerusalem stone somewhere; however, there just didn't seem to be a good place to put it. As we went out into the courtyard, I thought I would lay it on the ground, but there was security everywhere. I was simply placing a small Jerusalem stone outside the building, but I didn't want to be misconstrued by a security camera. They continued to herd the crowds toward the gate. I was praying, "Lord, where do you want me to place this stone?"

Just as we were going through the gate, I thought to myself, "I guess it's now or never!" I dropped the stone at the gate and kept walking. I made a proclamation under my breath. "Jerusalem is the throne of the Lord" (Jeremiah 3:17). That's when I heard the Holy Spirit say to me, "That's exactly where I wanted it, at the gate." I had proclaimed that Jerusalem is the government of God, not the United Nations. God would make the decisions that effect Israel and the world, not the United Nations. It was just my little prayer, offered in faith, but it was my small part in God's bigger picture.

As we rounded the corner of the building and stood across the street from the East River, as close as we could get, I pulled out my shofar, and blew it with all my might to proclaim that Jesus has the victory! God's will is going to be done for Israel and the world, no matter what man's government will try to do. Mission accomplished!

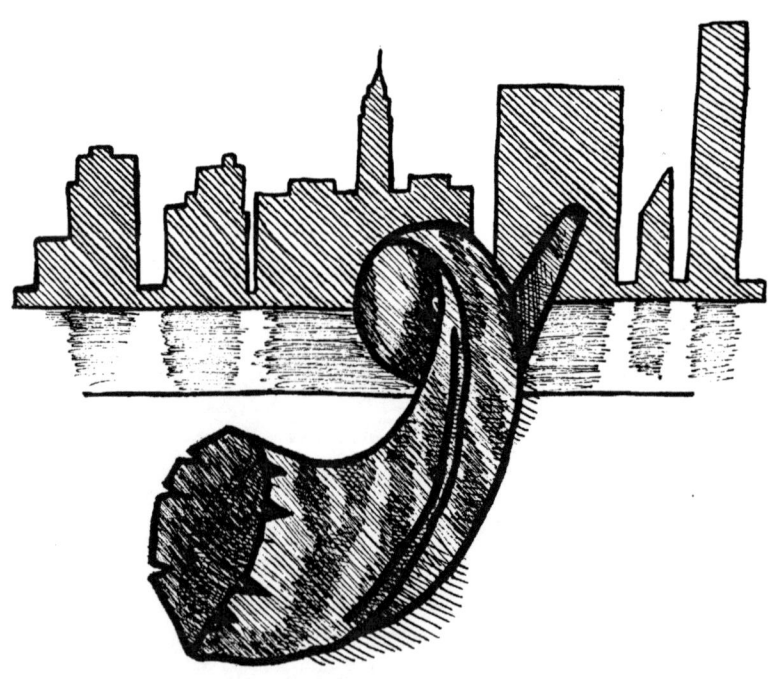

The Secret in the Wailing Wall

Who would have thought that a fifteen minute break at work and an "accidental" discovery on the library shelf would have taken me on an adventure around the world and back? That's the way it works when your life is an adventure with God. An ordinary occurrence can become a significant Kingdom event when God is leading your path and dropping clues for you to find. And, of course, if you are an astute spiritual sleuth!

I wandered into the library that day, at the First United Methodist Church where I was working as a secretary/receptionist. As a child, I was always drawn to dusty and musty old libraries. This was, after all, where I found adventure, particularly when I found my Nancy Drew books on the shelves! Now I was grown, but it always seemed that there was some mystery waiting to be discovered on a library shelf.

Little did I know what I would be finding on this particular day! I was looking over the choices, when my eye was drawn to a shelf with a very thick book called the *2004 Book of Resolutions*. I thought, "Hmmm…what is this?" I knew that the United Methodist Church had a *Book of Discipline*, from which the church drew it structure, but I had never heard of the *Book of Resolutions*.

I have always felt I was somehow supposed to find that book because when I flipped it open, and thumbed just a few pages through these documents that *supposedly* represent the whole of the beliefs of the United Methodists, immediately, my eyes fell upon these words: Number 312 "Opposition to Israeli Settlements in Palestinian Land." If I hadn't been learning all I had been over the previous years about Israel, and God's covenants with them for the land, and the miraculous way they became a nation in 1948, I might have missed the implications of this title. As I stood there, in that spot, and thought about it, I was suddenly struck by what this resolution was indeed saying.

"Opposition." *Opposition to what? What is the United Methodist Church opposing?* "Opposition to Israeli Settlements." *Wait, they are opposing Israeli settlements? Where?* "In Palestinian land." *Palestinian Land? Where is that? Oh, wait, that's Israel. Why are they calling Israel, Palestinian land? Let me think,* I said to myself, standing there in the library, glued to that spot. *They were saying that at least some portion of Israel's land doesn't belong to Israel, but were calling it by a different name. "Palestinian Land."*

I knew that the name "Palestine" was given to the land of Israel many hundreds of years before, by a conquering enemy ruler who wanted to insult the Jewish people by renaming their land after their enemies, the Philistines. I also knew that there are people known as Palestinians, and even Palestinian Christians, with whom God has great care and concern for their welfare, as well as the welfare of the Israelis. In addition, I had read that everyone who lived in Israel prior to 1948 were called "Palestinian," including Jews and Gentiles. It was only after the nation of Israel was established that Jewish people became known as modern-day "Israelis," and that the non-Jewish population in Israel were called Palestinians.

As I began to read the resolution, I was more and more in shock. *My denomination is asking Israel to do what?* I was reading words like "withdrawal," "Green Line," "dehumanizing checkpoints," etc. Something was not making sense to me. It seemed as if they were asking Israel to go backwards instead of forward, and to stop building and stop settling in the land that God had given them.

It seemed as though, unbelievably, they were asking the Israelis, not only to stop settling, but to give back land that I believed the Bible was saying belonged to Israel, and to which they had rightful modern-day ownership. The difficult part of it was that I realized that God loves and cares about the Palestinian people, too. The scripture that is most familiar to everyone says,

For God so loved the world, that He gave His only begotten Son, that whoever believes in Him shall not perish, but have eternal life (John 3:16).

Yes, I could see that this was a conflict of Biblical proportions; that had become evident to me, in particular, in those few moments of reading in that library. From all I had read in the Bible, I believed God had spoken concerning the nation and people of Israel, and that our modern-day dealings with them were to be done in a Biblical way, rather than in a politically correct way. My conviction was that if we were to do things according to God's order, then everyone would receive care, including the Palestinians. I didn't think I was being 'naive' to believe what the Bible says over man's ideas and opinions.

This discovery in the library began a personal campaign. I wanted to try to be a small drop in a very big pond, creating a ripple effect for change within the United Methodist Church and beyond. I decided to do what I could, which was to re-write this resolution. Of course, I realized that just re-writing it and even submitting it to the Alabama West Florida Conference of the United Methodist Church would not result in any type of immediate change. I knew there were processes that had to be observed for anything to happen, but I decided that even if just the words were read out loud, it could begin to change hearts and minds that were open. I felt that it might draw out those who believed the same way that I did, and that the Bible clearly shows God's everlasting and eternal covenant with Israel for the land (Psalm 105:6-15).

I sat down one night, with the help of the Holy Spirit, and re-wrote a mirror opposite resolution, based on what I believed the Bible to be saying. I titled it, "Support for Israeli Settlements in the Land of Israel." I had recently been asked to be a District Delegate for the Alabama West Florida Annual Conference, so I began a new process to see where this effort might lead. I began by submitting the resolution to my conference first.

I can remember the day I was going to submit the resolution. The deadline was already upon me, and I knew that I didn't have much time. I followed all the instructions given by the conference website on how to submit a resolution. When I hit "send," a momentary panic swept through me, knowing that I had just done something controversial, official, challenging, and it felt to me like, "in your face." I had no idea what would happen next. Would they throw it out? Would they let it go through? Would it be received in time to be published in that year's Annual Conference Brochure of Reports, the book that guides the proceedings each year? I soon found out when I received an e-mail, stating that they had received my resolution and it would indeed be published in the Brochure of Reports. It seemed that it would indeed be read by fifteen-hundred people or more. I was surprised at the passion that had risen up inside of me to do something that had the potential to really create a problem, but on the other hand, maybe could be a catalyst for change. I just knew that I had to move forward and see what might happen.

Annual Conference came that year and I can remember being so nervous about what was going to happen. I had been in much prayer and preparation of what I might say if I were given the chance to speak. The resolution didn't come up before the floor until the last day. The entire week had been spent discussing other matters on the agenda, and the Israel resolution was the last thing to be brought to the table for discussion. There was something very prophetic to me about the fact that this issue was last, emphasizing how far away we were from the mark. It seemed to me that we needed to get to the place of Israel being our first priority in prayer and actions as Christians, since the gospel is to the Jew first (Romans 1:16).

I had been warned that the committee had to first concur or non-concur, (basically, agree or disagree) and that they would probably non-concur. This turned out to be the case. The committee gave their recommendation of "non-concurrence," which meant that they did not agree with the resolution I had written because it was too much of an opposing viewpoint to the United Methodist Church's current position on Israel. The floor was then opened for discussion.

This is the part I really do love about the Methodist church. It is not a dictatorship. Everyone is given the freedom to choose and decide and walk with God from where they are. Everyone has a right to speak. It is much like the democratic system of government in our nation. That freedom can be for good or bad, but everyone is given the right to speak and take action, and to vote.

My honest feeling is that everyone was too tired after a long week at conference, discussing insurance and such, and were ready to be finished by the time this Israel resolution came up. Most of them had a two to four hour drive ahead of them to get home that day. I felt like perhaps by that time, no one was in the mood to discuss Middle East politics. However, in fairness to the process, it had to be discussed.

The question was asked by the committee if anyone wanted to speak concerning this proposed resolution. I remember in a room full of approximately fifteen-hundred to two-thousand people, one man went up to the microphone and said that he disagreed with my resolution, for various reasons, but mainly because he had some Palestinian friends whom he didn't think would like it.

The Bishop asked if there was anyone else who wanted to speak. I waited for a second, and didn't see any hands raised of people who wanted to speak. I jumped on it, and raised mine. I was given permission to go to the microphone. I was very confident, although I felt nervous, as I could hear the sound of my own feet tapping on the floor. The room was silent.

At that point, I identified myself as the writer of the resolution, and began to share with everyone why I had written it. I quoted from Psalm 105:6-15 which states:

> *O seed of Abraham, His servant, O sons of Jacob, His chosen ones! He is the Lord our God; His judgments are in all the earth.* **He has remembered His covenant forever,** *the word which He commanded to* **a thousand generations,** *the covenant which he made with Abraham, and his oath to Isaac. Then He confirmed it to Jacob for a statute, to Israel as an everlasting covenant, saying,* **"To you I will give the**

land of Canaan as the portion of your inheritance," *When they were only a few men in number. Very few, and strangers in it. And they wandered about from nation to nation, from one kingdom to another people. He permitted no man to oppress them, and he reproved kings for their sakes. "Do not touch My anointed ones, and do My prophets no harm." [my emphasis]*

I pointed out that the promise was specifically through the line of Jacob, which was Israel. Jacob, of course, was the father of the twelve tribes of Israel. I then shared with them about General Edmund Allenby, who was used by God to release Jerusalem from Turkish control in 1917. As a Christian, his mother taught him to pray for God's people, Israel, every night before he went to bed. And the prayer was: *"And O Lord, we would not forget your ancient people Israel. Hasten the day when Israel shall again be your people and be restored to Your favor and to their land."* Then Allenby said, *"I never knew God would give me the privilege of answering my own childhood prayer."*[6]

After I finished, I went back to my seat, waiting for the next person to go to the microphone. No one did. There was no one who went to speak up for Israel. I was shocked, even though when I wrote the resolution, I didn't really expect it to pass. I had written it originally, just knowing that the words being read and discussed and voted on, would at least have an effect of allowing others to hear what the Bible says about Israel.

The vote was finally taken, and only about 10% of the hands went up in favor of my resolution. Suddenly, I felt crushed. It had nothing to do with me, or that I felt personally rejected, because I didn't. I just felt so broken-hearted for Israel, and also for the Methodist Church, that they seemed to me to be on the wrong side of a very important issue in these days that we live in. The whole world is coming against Israel, and now, we as a denomination, were also coming against them. This made me very sad. I had to get up and leave the room and go to the courtyard at the church to try and collect myself.

---

6   Dr. Richard Booker, *The Time to Favor Zion has Come*, p. 21 (quoting Ed Vallowe, *The Budding of the Fig Tree*, p. 73).

I decided at that point not to give up. I knew that in 2008, the General Conference of the United Methodist Church (worldwide) would meet in Texas. This was the actual conference who voted in the resolutions and petitions. There would be one thousand or so delegates there, and they would have to read out loud and discuss the resolution if I sent it in. This was where, in 2004, Resolution #312, had passed, and had become the official United Methodist Church's stand against Israeli settlements on what they felt was Palestinian land. Although I knew I wouldn't be there, because I wasn't a General Conference delegate, I decided I would send it anyway. I also knew there was only a very slim chance of it passing, since it was in direct opposition to the resolution that they had voted in at General Conference four years previously.

In October, 2007, before all this happened, I had the opportunity to go to Israel. I was very excited to go since this was my first time, but as I was preparing for the trip, I felt there was something I must do. I packed into my suitcase the resolution I had written even though I wasn't sure I would be able to accomplish what I felt I should do. But I had to try. I was able to first have my friends pray over the resolution, and anoint it with oil. I then went to the Wailing Wall in Jerusalem, along with all the others who were making a pilgrimage there, to pray with the resolution in my hand!

I stood there, on the woman's side, and placed the anointed and prayed-over resolution into a large crack at the bottom of the wall, along with so many other rolled up prayer requests. It was an awesome moment for me. I felt like the heaven and earth may have shifted that day, at least in my own world. I felt like in some way this was making my own piece of history. I was taking a piece of paper, in which I had written down the way I felt things should be according to my understanding of the Bible, and put it into this wall, revered by many as the holiest physical site on earth.

Then, in April, 2008, it was time for General Conference, where I had submitted the resolution. It was read, along with many other resolutions covering a wide range of topics. That was also the particular year in which the United Methodist Church was trying to divest money from Israel. That did not happen, thankfully, but this was an indication of the atmosphere within the United Methodist Church worldwide, concerning Israel. I watched the progression of the voting which was taking place, from my home computer, as I went on line to check every day to see if it has passed. Again, it did not pass. Out of one thousand or so delegates, 38 voted in favor of my resolution.

I realized that, at least for the time being, that I was to rest from all of it, until God showed me what to do next. It would be another three years before I picked it up again, quite unexpectedly. For now, I was satisfied to know that the words of truth from the Bible had been read out loud in my own United Methodist Annual Conference, as well as the General Conference, the main governing body of our denomination.

I believe that the United Methodist Church does have many good characteristics. I have a love for the United Methodists that was put there by God. I just believe that we have gotten off track as it relates to Israel and other issues, but the Lord is always in the process of restoration. He is "restoring the land and the people to Israel." That is a play on words that has several meanings. It is the sub-title for *East River Ministries*. It means restoring the land of Israel back to their original owners, the children of Abraham, Isaac and Jacob, which are the Jewish people. It means restoring the Jewish people back to their own land of Israel. This is called aliyah, which means, "to go up." In the literal sense this means the Jewish immigration to Israel.

There is also a restoring of the people of the church back to their Jewish roots and into a love for the Jewish people and the land of Israel. I see the word aliyah also as meaning "coming up higher," as we come to recognize Israel's place in God's plan of redemption, and make it a priority of prayer. There is also a restoring of all people in a spiritual sense, both Jew and Gentile, through salvation that comes through the Jewish Messiah, Yeshua/Jesus.

When I placed that resolution titled, "Support for Israeli Settlements in the Land of Israel," into that crack in the Wailing

Wall in Jerusalem, I felt I was putting a prayer of many people right up close to the heartbeat of God, and He heard this prayer along with the prayers of many others. Eventually, all things will be restored.

A Surprise Encounter on the Temple Mount

I've attended church since I was a child. My mother and father had me baptized into the Lutheran denomination as a baby. I really do not ever remember a time that we did not get up on Sunday mornings and go to church. Many mornings, on the way to Sunday school, we would see little children out playing in their yards in their regular play clothes. Every time, my mother would comment with the saddest sound in her voice, "Oh, look at those poor little children who don't get to go to Sunday school and hear about Jesus."

My brother and I would look sadly out the back window of the car and watch them play as we continued driving. If I had a hint of envy that they were outside playing and we were in a car on the way to a long morning in church, it was overshadowed by the pity that I felt in my heart for them.

This experience set the stage for how I would feel many years later when I was in Israel, and God gave me a sense of mercy and compassion for some other children that I saw there. Our tour group was headed to the Temple Mount in Jerusalem. This was the part that I had looked most forward to during our twelve-day journey.

I was preparing myself for the incredible emotions that I knew I would feel when I went to the Wailing Wall. I knew I would feel these emotions, not only for my personal experience of prayer that I would have there, but also because what I knew I would see. I had already seen images on TV of the Jewish people, particularly the men, davening (rocking back and forth in prayer), in their black hats and tallits (prayer shawls). I also knew that there would be an overwhelming sense of being one with everyone who had been there, as I observed the many prayer requests in the cracks of the wall, while adding my own.

As we made our way through the security checks, we were taken across scaffolding that was over the top of new archaeological digs that were happening on the Temple Mount. We were able, from that vantage point, to look down and see the familiar scenes that I had seen on TV and in pictures. I did feel a sense of awe as I was finally seeing for the first time something that was such a part of my Biblical heritage. I did have an incredibly moving time in prayer as we finally made our way to the wall itself.

As meaningful as that was, it was another incident on the Temple Mount, however, that stands out in my mind. It was one that I did not expect, and when it happened, I knew I had just experienced an encounter with God. The incident I refer to happened as we were in the Arab section of the Temple Mount in front of the huge Dome of the Rock. This is a Muslim shrine, and is one of the main sources of the conflict in the Middle East.

This site is believed by Jewish people to be the exact location that Abraham offered his son Isaac to the Lord, but the Lord stayed his hand and he did not have to carry out the sacrifice. This is also where Solomon's Temple stood when the Jewish nation was at its most significant time in its history. On the other hand, the Muslim people believe that it was not Isaac, but Ishmael, Abraham's first son, who was being offered. The Muslims also believe that this was the location from which Mohammed ascended to heaven. Therefore, the site is important to both people groups.

We were passing by the Dome of the Rock site when I saw something that touched my heart. As I was standing there with my tour group while they were purchasing items from Arab traders, I witnessed a very large group of Muslim school children coming out onto the cobblestone courtyard. They were all dressed alike, boys wearing blue and girls wearing pink. They each had a little backpack and they were being guided by their teachers - Muslim women wearing their long dresses and headscarves.

As I watched this group of school children, my emotions were stirred, just as they had been so long ago when my mother used to point out the children who did not get to go to Sunday school. I cannot fully describe all that went through my mind in those moments of watching these hundred or so Muslim children and their teachers. The compassion I felt for them was overwhelming, and I stood there weeping and watching them. They were so truly beautiful.

My first thought was how sad it seemed that they lived in a world with so much violence and hatred. They looked so innocent, simply believing what they were being taught. It was not by their choice that they had been born into their religion, as is the case with most people, although ultimately we must make our own decisions about matters of faith. It made me wonder why it seemed that some people had the inside understanding of the truth of the gospel of Jesus and others didn't. It seemed as if God had made a sovereign choice that was difficult to understand. He loves all of His creation.

I certainly don't have all the answers to these things, but it did give me an appreciation of seeing the other side of the coin. I was watching the people whom I had come to see in my mind as enemies, and suddenly, I was seeing them with new eyes, as people created in God's image. They were going about their everyday lives, working, going to school, having lunch, worshiping and praying.

I was sad for them, most of all, because they did not know the one true and living God. Those Arab Muslim people on the eastern side of Jerusalem, praying near the Dome of the Rock, did not know Jesus. For that matter, neither did the Jewish men and women praying on the western side of Jerusalem at the Wailing Wall. The same could be said of some of those of the Christian religion who did not know Jesus in a personal way, but were going through rituals. All religions are guilty in various ways of trusting in rituals for salvation, rather than simply trusting in Jesus' perfect sacrifice for the sins of the whole world. John 3:16, the most beloved scripture in the Bible, certainly applies here.

All of those ancient stones were there, as if hearing the prayers of the many men, women and children over the years, prayers for peace, prayers for the Messiah to come, and prayers for countless other things.

Evan Levine sings a song called, "May the God of Israel Reign," which moves me very deeply every single time I hear it, because I am envisioning what I saw on the Temple Mount that day. The words to the song are:

These stone walls are crying out for truth,
Let it wail in the streets, and burn in the youth,
These stone walls, with prayers left in their cracks,
He will hear your prayer for peace, when His people turn back,
Amayn and Amayn, may the God of Israel reign...[7]

– Evan Levine

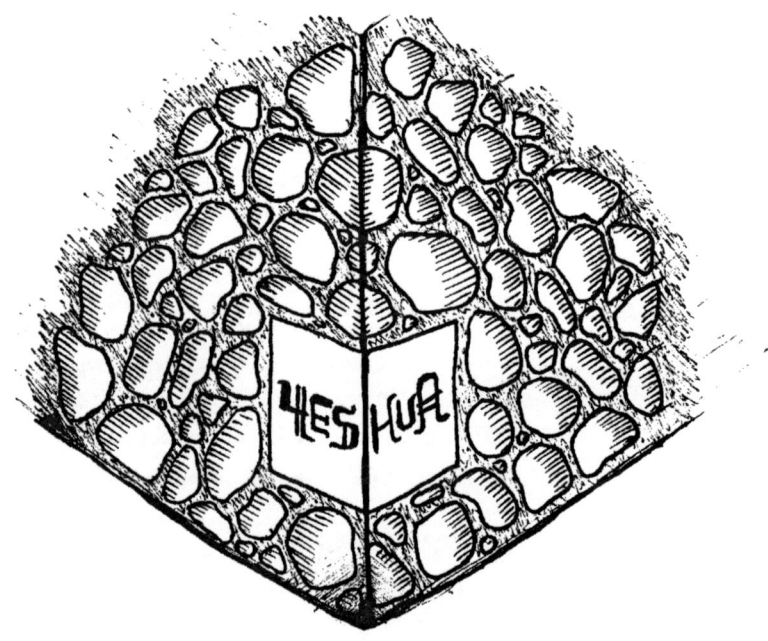

---

[7] *For Zion's Sake I Will Not Be Silent* – Ted Pearce - 2007

As I saw that day, the multitudes of people praying, rocking (davening) back and forth, or kneeling on mats with their shoes off, or going through ritualistic liturgies and ceremonies, it was as if the stones were crying out for the truth that Jesus (Yeshua), the Jewish and Gentile Messiah, the God of Israel, has already come, and was missed by many, but He is coming again to rule and to reign.

Revelation 5:9-10 reveals a scene from heaven which is very profound.

And they sang a new song, saying, "Worthy are You to take the book and to break its seals; for You were slain, and purchased for God with Your blood men from every tribe and tongue and people and nation.

You have made them to be a kingdom and priests to our God; and they will reign upon the earth.

I couldn't help but think of the scriptures in Acts 4:11-23:

He is the stone which was rejected by you, the builders, but which became the chief corner stone. And there is salvation in no one else; **for there is no other name under heaven that has been given among men by which we must be saved** *(vv. 11-12, my emphasis).*

It will happen someday. All the nations of the world will worship the Lord, Jesus the Messiah. He is the true Prince of Peace, and real peace (shalom) will come only through Him. In the meantime, it is our responsibility to do as Psalm 122:6 says,

Pray for the peace of Jerusalem...

The Mystery of the Dove in the Barbed Wire

This story is about my second trip to New York City that related to Israel and the Jewish people. It is also about the incredible things we uncovered while there for the 60th anniversary celebration of the Nation of Israel at the United Nations. (The first trip is explained in the chapter entitled, *Danger in New York City*.) On that trip there were nine of us going as a team. On this second trip, there were only four, but we really learned some significant things that need to be shared.

We had heard that Robert Stearns, a Christian singer and speaker, was going to be hosting a banquet at the United Nations with Jewish people and Christian people together for Israel's 60th anniversary. Since I could not be in Israel for this momentous occasion, I felt compelled to go to the New York City event.

The four of us decided that it would just be an extraordinary thing to be in the place that the nation of Israel was birthed in 1948, even though in today's time, the United Nations is not on Israel's side, but is constantly trying to get Israel to concede land for peace, etc. That's why it was amazing to me that this event would even be held there. Just prior to this time, the President of Iran and others were still allowed to come to the UN and say whatever they wanted to about Israel, which was never good. Being there felt a little like being in the belly of the beast. (Interpret that how you will.)

The event itself was spectacular, with a host of Jewish and Christian personalities speaking, like John Hagee, Pat Boone, Rabbi

Shlomo Riskin, and others. It gave me chills to see us all standing together in support of the nation of Israel.

It was during our time in New York City that we discovered some interesting things about the United Methodist Church's position on Israel. I feel that there are some things that need to be exposed for everyone to understand.

Just as many times the United States seems to comply with the United Nations bureaucrats, and makes decisions that the average person has no idea about, the United Methodist Church also, in the upper echelons, makes decisions that the average lay person in the church knows nothing about, and we assume that all is well. Perhaps it would benefit us as citizens and lay people to discover some of the policies that our country and our denominations hold forth, things which are put into place while we are asleep.

It is not my intent to come against everything that the United Methodist Women's organization does, or that the United Methodist Church does. My main concern in the writing of this book is to explain my understanding of where they stand in regards to Israel. As I mention throughout this book, I have a great love for the United Methodist Church overall, and I think they have done a lot of things right. However, I have a serious concern over their policies on Israel.

When we were in NYC, one of the places we visited was 777 United Nations Plaza. This is the twelve-story Church Center for the United Nations, which houses the Women's Division of the UMC offices, the United Methodist Board of Church and Society office, as well as offices of other denominations. This building is directly across from the United Nations and is owned by the United Methodist Church.

We felt that we needed to go to this building to take a tour to look around and see what we could find out. There was a doorman in the lobby who welcomed us. We explained that we were a group of Methodists from Florida, Alabama and California who wanted to see the headquarters of the United Methodist Women. He called upstairs and got permission for us to come up.

A very nice woman greeted us and offered to give us a tour around the United Methodist Womens' office. She explained to us how things happened day to day, and what kinds of work they do. We were asking her questions and enjoying the experience of seeing this place that has such a powerful influence within the United Methodist Church.

She took us to a room and we went out onto a balcony. From there we could see the front entrance to the United Nations with all its flags of the nations, directly across the street. She began explaining to us that the building we were in was built and paid for by the United Methodist Women in the early 1960s. She told us that they had strategically chosen that site because they wanted to work closely with the United Nations on policies. I was a little taken aback by this. To know that the location was chosen for that very reason, and realizing how closely related their procedures were, it made me realize the power of influence.

"Who influences who more?" I asked her. "Does the United Methodist Women influence the United Nations more, or does the United Nations influence the United Methodist Women more?"

"We influence each other equally," she replied.

That was a statement I have never forgotten. The reason I have never forgotten it is because I realized that since the United Methodist Women helps to shape the current thought process of the United Methodist Church on Israel, and because they were working with the United Nations to persuade Israel to give away their land that God gave them, this could not be good.

I knew that they had written some literature that was making the church see Israel in the way that they thought was right; however, rather than being Biblical in their literature, it seemed to me that they were more concerned with being politically correct.

This influence happens from the top, and trickles down. In other words, the United Methodist Women's Division based in New York City writes literature that flows down into the local church groups, where unsuspecting lay people read it and form their own opinions. One example of this was the Israel/Palestine Study, which was very biased literature that many believe painted an unfair picture of Israel. This is why it is so important for us as individuals to be grounded in the Word of God on these subjects. We should never just blindly take the opinions of people, but always check them against strong Biblical interpretation.

As we were leaving, we were coming through a hallway when we noticed a large poster on the wall. It took me by surprise, although by that time, it really shouldn't have. It was a picture of a white dove wrapped in barbed wire. The message on the poster read, "End the Illegal Occupation of Palestine."

If there was ever a doubt in my mind that the United Methodist Church sees Israel in a bad light, I certainly did not doubt it now. The resolution that I have tried to battle against, Number 312, which, again, is entitled, "Opposition to Israeli Settlements in Palestinian Land" clearly states that the United Methodist Church wants us to stop supporting Israel's rights to her God-given land, and this poster magnified that way of thinking. I found out later that this poster was a product of the World Council of Churches, an organization also based in New York City, which seeks Christian unity among many denominations.

Let me make my voice heard. I do not believe that Israel is illegally occupying her own land. From my own research of both Biblical and modern history, I believe that it belongs to them, given by God. I discuss the Biblical foundations for this in various places throughout this book. Isaiah 66:8 asks the question, "Can a nation be born in a day?" A positive answer would seem impossible, however, in the case of Israel, the answer was miraculously, "Yes." The modern history of Israel can be summed up in the fact that Israel was born out of the fires of the Holocaust. It was a nation that was voted in legally by the delegates from the nations of the world at the United Nations assembly in 1948.

Immediately, they were attacked by surrounding Arab nations who stated that they wanted to wipe Israel off the map. Israel was originally happy to have the land they were given, but when they were attacked, they had to defend themselves and their newly formed state. This resulted in more territory being taken out of necessity. Israel offered their enemies land for peace many times, but they refused because they were not content to have Israel's presence at all.

Furthermore, I believe the Bible is very clear that we are not to touch the apple of God's eye. In fact, I believe it would help if we, as a church, would stand in identificational repentance for the United Nations, the United States, and the United Methodist Church, as well as Christianity in general, for the way we have treated Israel.

As we left those offices, we rode the elevator back down to the ground floor and were still in shock over what we had just seen. Our worst fears had been confirmed, that the denomination that we love so much and to which we are a part, is against Israel and thinks of them as illegally occupying their own land. They also think of Israel as enforcers, sometimes even making them seem like Nazis, trying to push innocent people around.

While I realize that Israel is certainly far from perfect, and have made some mistakes, for the most part in order to protect and defend their own country. We, as the United States of America, would do no less for our own, and I'm sure we would welcome Israel's support to defend us if it were needed.

We went into the chapel before we left the building. Again, I was unprepared for what I saw. Although this building is the Church Center for the United Nations, I was still expecting a chapel built by the United Methodist Church to be Christian oriented. On the wall, over the altar were five symbols of various faiths. To the far left, there was a cross, then a Jewish star, then a Muslim crescent, and then two other symbols I didn't recognize. It was an interfaith chapel. Something just felt wrong to me about that. Jesus was no longer front and center, one and only. He was lined up and on equal grounds as other religions. He had been dethroned. The four of us joined in prayer together that day in the chapel.

Before we left, we did do one last thing. We had brought with us a beautiful picture that a friend of mine, Marylin Funchess, had drawn. It was an eye with a Star of David right where the pupil normally would be. This picture gave the message that Israel is indeed the apple of God's eye. I took it and laid it atop the open bible on the pulpit. I wanted to remind those who might see it of where we are to keep our focus when praying for the nations of the world.

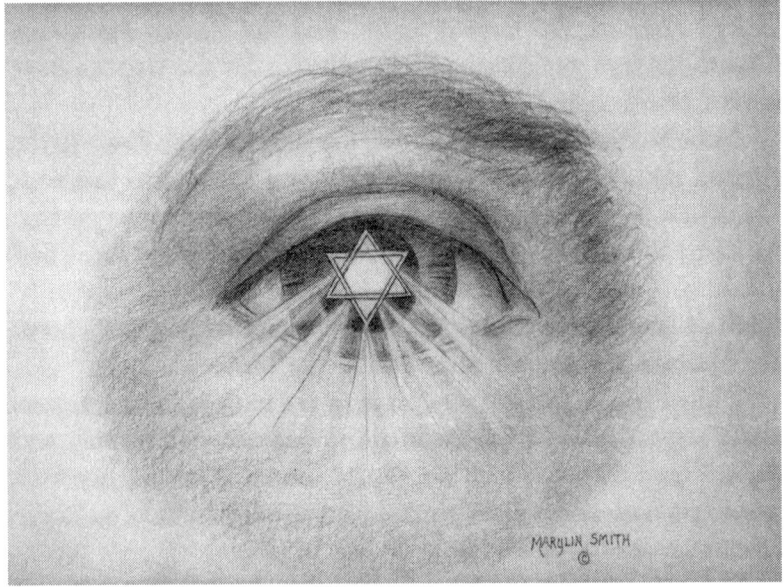

The Case of the Mysterious Poll-Taker

It was June and time for the United Methodist Church Annual Conference 2009 for Alabama West Florida. I had prayed about what I could do to be an influence for Israel. I had not been able to secure a table to share information that would further my cause. I felt I must get creative in my approach. The idea came to me to take a poll to raise awareness. I did not have official permission but felt like it would be fine if I just quietly asked a few questions of some of the pastors and lay delegates.

I walked around undetected the entire weekend. I only let myself be known to those that I felt the Lord directed. I truly felt like a spiritual sleuth, or somewhat of an undercover detective. It was fun and exciting, but actually quite serious. When I began asking questions, the answers I was receiving were giving me a good picture of the pulse of our Annual Conference concerning Israel.

It was interesting to me that June of 2009 also happened to be 42nd anniversary of the liberation of Jerusalem in 1967, which made it the capital of the Jewish state of Israel. With clipboard and pen in hand, I wandered through the crowd of about two-thousand people.

"Excuse me," I would begin. "Would you mind if I asked you a few questions concerning Israel?" Nearly everyone said, "Yes!"

Question #1: Did the Holocaust Really Happen?

Question #2: Could a modern-day holocaust of Jews and/or Christians still happen today?

It was shocking to me to get home one day later and hear these words in the headlines: **Guard Killed by a white Neo-Nazi** supremacist at the Holocaust Memorial Museum in Washington DC. This modern-day Neo-Nazi is quoted to have said he believed the holocaust never really happened.

How ironic. How thought-provoking. I wish I could have polled more people, but the answers I did get from those polled were very revealing of what those in our Annual Conference really believe.

The reason I did the poll was two-fold. First, I wanted to find out if the lay people and local clergy are in any way in agreement with the official stand about Israel from the United Methodist Church's book of Resolutions. What I found was amazing. Nearly eighty percent of Clergy and Lay people polled did not know what their own denomination believes about the land and the people of Israel. I was one of these unsuspecting lay people, until the day that I discovered the *Book of Resolutions* and found Resolution Number 312, quite by accident, although I do believe it was more of God's providence that I did find it.

The second reason I did the poll was that I hoped to raise awareness and thought-provoking questions about the beloved land and people of Israel.

This is not really about politics. It's about the Kingdom of God and the return of Jesus to Jerusalem, and the covenant promises of God to the Jewish people leading up to these events.

I hoped that the headline news that came out the day after I got home from Annual Conference about the Neo-Nazi shooting at the Holocaust Museum would underline the importance of why we need to make it our business to know what our denomination believes about such an important subject.

For anyone who is interested, the subject can be found in the *Book of Resolutions*, 2004 and 2008, Resolution #312. "Opposition to Israeli Settlements in Palestinian Land."

No one has a problem seeing that the views of a white, Neo-Nazi supremacist are anti-Semitic and just plain wrong. I believe, however, that the United Methodist Church is unknowingly displaying a more subtle form of anti-Semitism. Thankfully though, within the Alabama West-Florida Conference, what I found through the poll was that at the very least there were approximately forty-eight percent who did believe that Israel has a right to their own land. Others were not sure what they believed so they declined to answer.

The lay people and clergy, for the most part, don't know that these sentiments exist within the United Methodist Church! Those whom I talked to assumed that our denomination did support Israel. Most members of the United Methodist Church whom I have shared this story with were as shocked as I was to find out this information.

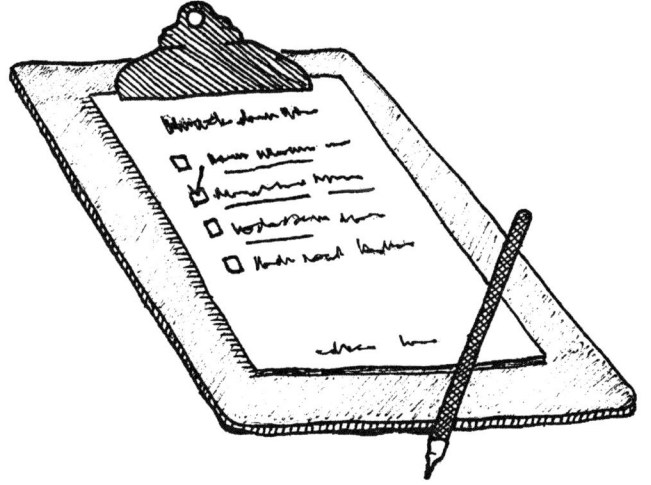

I know that it will not be easy to change this. I know because I tried re-writing resolution #312 in 2007. Mine was a mirror-opposite. Instead of "Opposition to Israeli Settlements in Palestinian Land," the resolution I wrote said, "Support for Israeli Settlements in the Land of Israel." It was rejected at the Alabama West Florida Conference in 2007, as well as at General Conference in 2008.

"We must remain vigilant against anti-Semitism in all its forms." This is a quote from President Obama. I listened to him on the news talking about the incident at the Holocaust museum. He was horrified by what happened. However, is it not a form of anti-Semitism for him to pressure the Jewish people to give up their land to the Palestinians? He, as well as the United Methodist Church and many others, says that it is in the name of "peace." They say it is for the Jewish people to have a state, and the Palestinian people to have a state.

Remember, however, what happened in 2005 when the United States government pressured Israel to pull their own people out of Gaza to give the land to the Palestinians? What was once a lush and fertile strip of land when the Israelis lived there, within a short time was demolished by fighting of terrorist factions from within. That same strip of land then became a launching pad for thousands of rockets into Israel. Israel ultimately had to defend itself, an action for which the United Methodists and many others are still blaming Israel.

In my opinion, a two-state solution can't be the answer. We should not pressure Israel to give up land for a man-made peace. First of all, is there not a dark force who wants to drive Israel into the sea? How can we think that if Israel gives up any more land that they are going to have peace? Gaza paints the picture of what will result if further land is relinquished.

Do we remember, or have we forgotten why the State of Israel came into existence? It was birthed out of the fires of the Holocaust. The Jewish people needed their own safe-place to return, which turned out to be the place ordained by God for them from the beginning.

Did the Holocaust really happen? It most definitely did. One hundred percent of those who took the poll agreed on that!

Could a modern day Holocaust of Jews and/or Christians happen today? If we look at the actions of James Von Brunn, the Neo-Nazi white supremacist who killed that guard, we might see that it is possible. If he and people like him were to have their way, the answer is probably more like, "most definitely."

Why is this subject not a top priority within our Annual Conferences as well as the greater United Methodist Church and, in fact, all denominations? The United Methodist Church is not the only one. I'm just wondering if those of us who love and support and bless Israel and the Jewish people could come together. Can we start a grass-roots movement to change the official stand of the United Methodist Church and other Protestant denominations that are against Israel? All we need is one smooth stone to knock down the Goliath! That smooth stone would be faith in Almighty God to answer our prayers when we join together, taking action.

The Clue of the Delegate Badge

This little story is actually a combination addendum to "The Clue in the Wailing Wall" and "Danger in New York City." This has to do with our calling as the church to act in the spirit of modern day Esthers and Mordecais, who will stand for God's people, Israel in the face of a real spirit of a modern-day Haman, the enemy of God's people.

Between 2008 and 2010, I had been in a time of real soul-searching, trying to understand what I was to do next, if anything, in this calling on my life concerning Israel and the Jewish people. I asked myself continually if I had done everything I felt I was supposed to do. Since I had not had any more promptings from the Lord, I was nearly ready to lay everything down concerning pressing the United Methodist Church to change their ways concerning Israel, but apparently God was not finished with me quite yet.

I had been cleaning out a bedroom and making it into an office, when I made a discovery. It might not have been obvious to others, but when God shows you something, it is usually based on things that would make sense only to you, because He knows each of us intimately.

I had cleaned out the entire bedroom and the room was nearly in place, but one morning as I walked into the room I noticed two things lying together on the floor. They were highlighted to me, as if a beam of light from heaven was shining down on them. One of the items was my delegate badge, which I had worn to a previous conference for the Alabama West Florida Conference. At first I thought, "I will pick that up and put it away," but then I looked closer.

The other item was a package from a small bottle of anointing oil that was made by my friend Cynthia who is an apothecary and travels in and out of Israel and gathers things to make wonderful scented oils. This particular oil was called "Esther." There was a little paper with a picture of Queen Esther on the front, which explained the symbolism and meaning of the oil.

When I saw these two items lying together, I stopped everything. I was struck by the thought in that very moment, that God was calling me again, to stand in for Israel as an Esther, similar to the way I had done in New York City. This time, it was at the Alabama West Florida Annual Conference. I knew in that moment that I was to write another resolution.

I began immediately to write that for Israel. This time, I didn't use the same format as I had in 2007, when I had written a mirror opposite to the resolution that was already in place within the *Book of Resolutions*. Now, I thought I should change my approach by simply writing something that I felt would line up with the scriptures about Israel. It would be something that I hoped would be difficult for the Committee on Petitions and Resolutions and the conference to refuse.

As I began to write, what started out to be one resolution became two, each with their own strong messages. Both addressed two timely and difficult subjects. The first one was called, "Resolution on Israel and Replacement Theology." The second one was called, "Resolution on the Jewish People and Anti-Semitism."

A brief explanation of Replacement Theology is this: It is the thinking that since the Jewish people rejected Jesus, the church has now replaced Israel in the plans and purposes of God. Replacement Theology sees no need to focus on a restored national Israel as a fulfillment of Bible prophecy.

My son, Nick, who was a creative writing major and was just graduating, helped me to polish them up to make the message of these resolutions as understandable and grammatically accurate as possible. In fact, it was Nick who suggested that I actually needed to make them two resolutions instead of one.

I went through the process of submitting them to the Committee on Petitions and Resolutions as I had done before. I was concerned that I did not get them into the office in time; however, they did make it, and they were added as the very last items in the Brochure of Reports, which was to be read, discussed and voted on during the conference.

The moment of truth arrived earlier this time than it had when I submitted the earlier resolution in 2007. The conference, which normally goes from Sunday to Wednesday, had much business to discuss, and I remembered that the resolution I had written in 2007 didn't come up until Wednesday. This time it came up on Monday morning. I was feeling more confident this time, because I had worded the resolutions in such a way, I hoped, that they could not be disputed.

Again, to my surprise, the Committee on Resolutions and Petitions had voted to non-concur with the first of the two resolutions, just as they had when I had done this in 2007. The first one for 2010 was the resolution on Israel and Replacement Theology. The committee's explanation for disagreement was that the resolution was not in line with the current resolutions of the United Methodist Church regarding Israel. They said that the resolution I had written was only one way of looking at the scriptures, and that they didn't want to lock everyone into seeing those scriptures in that same way. I found that interesting, since the Resolutions on Israel, especially #312, which are already in place in the *Book of Resolutions*, do just that. The amazing thing is that the average United Methodist lay person is clueless, since these things are decided at the General Conference which meets every four years, with a delegation of representatives from all over the world.

The invitation was then given to the delegates, a representation of the six hundred and fifty or so churches in our conference, to come to the microphone if they would like to speak for or against my resolution. Once again, as I had done in 2007, I waited for a few moments, and realized that no one was going to get up to go to the microphone. I raised my hand and was given the signal to come share whatever I wanted.

After identifying myself as the writer of the resolution, I began by reminding everyone of the rising tide of anti-Semitism which is taking place throughout the world. I told them that I hoped that our conference would be different from the rest of the United Methodist Church, since after all, most of us were evangelical and lived in an area of the country which is known for its more conservative values. I did my best to rally the conference into action, to be a first among all the United Methodist Church conferences who would have a pro-Israel stand.

As part of my speech, I shared something that I had discovered in my research. Abram Mordecai was a Jewish man who was the *first* settler of Montgomery County in the 1700's. Montgomery is where our Annual Conference is held every year. It seemed appropriate to me that we should also be a *first* in speaking up concerning Israel. I found it interesting that his name was Mordecai, who is also the older cousin and adopted "father" in the story of Esther, who prompted her to go before the king on behalf of her people, the Jews. I related to this story because of how I had found the Esther anointing oil previously mentioned.

Abram Mordecai was converted to Christianity and became part of the Methodist denomination. He had heard preaching by a circuit rider across the river, which led to his conversion. In those days, the Methodists rode their circuits on horses, roaming from town-to-town, sharing the gospel.[8]

I reminded the group of pastors and lay people at Annual Conference that according to Romans 1:16, the gospel is for the "Jew first," and that I hoped we would be the *first* conference to place the Jewish people as a priority by voting for the resolutions. If the resolutions were to pass in the Alabama-West Florida

---

8 http://www.archives.state.al.us/al_sldrs/m_list.html

Conference, this would not change the overall stand of the United Methodist Church on Israel, but would be a start where we could possibly have a groundswell toward change.

When it came time to vote, there weren't enough hands going up for it to pass, but there seemed to be many more than when I had written the resolution in 2007. The next one, "Resolution on the Jewish People and Anti-Semitism" came up for vote. This time, I felt pretty sure it would pass; After all, who would be in favor of anti-Semitism? The question was asked if anyone would like to say anything. I waited. My pastor's wife, Garilyn, sitting next to me, raised her yellow card to indicate that she would like to speak. It was as if she were invisible. No one seemed to see her, and before we knew what happened, the vote was taking place. Again, there were a good number of hands who voted in favor of this resolution that the committee had non-concurred with, but still not enough for it to pass. Their reason for non-concurrence on this one was something along these lines; while they were definitely against anti-Semitism, they were non-concurring for mostly the same reasons as the first resolution. With those words, the vote was over and done in less than two minutes.

I sat there, frozen for a little while. I tried to stay as they voted in favor of standing against gambling, and other issues, but I could no longer focus. As I sat there, thinking about what to do next, a man came right up to me, into the aisle.

"Are you the one who just spoke about Israel?" he asked.

"Yes."

"I want you to know," he said, "that you did the right thing, and I agree with you. I had no idea the Methodist church felt this way about Israel, and I am shocked. I cannot stay here. These are not my people." After a few more words of encouraging me, he walked out the back door.

A swirl of emotions was going through my mind! I had just been knocked down, and then immediately encouraged tremendously, all within about ten minutes. After I gathered my thoughts, I got up and went out the back door. I saw the gentleman, sitting across the lobby, with the opened Brochure of Reports on his lap, reading my resolution on the very last page.

I walked around outside to calm myself. I was thinking, "Well, I supposed it is really over with. I suppose I've done everything I can do." God, however, had other plans.

As I walked back into the building, I saw him still sitting there. He seemed to be finished reading, and I sensed that perhaps he did not know what to do next. I walked up to him and thanked him for what he said to me. I thanked him for standing with me and for encouraging me. I told him that I really knew that God had sent him as an encouragement. He was still full of emotions and even anger, and rightfully so. This time, I found myself encouraging him. I told him that maybe if we quit too soon, nothing would ever change. Maybe there was a job to do now, and perhaps we were supposed to stay and work toward change.

Suddenly, another man approached. He said he wanted to thank me for writing the resolution and speaking out about Israel. I was floored. He said that he and his wife had seen the resolution the night before in their hotel room and had been praying that it would pass. When it didn't, he was very upset and knew that his wife would be, too. The three of us stood there, probably close to an hour, discussing what we should do. We determined in our hearts that we should not automatically leave, just because the voting did not go in the way we hoped it would. We all agreed that we loved the United Methodist Church, and wanted to see people gain an understanding of why we should stand with and support Israel.

I turned and saw my Pastor Alan Ferguson and his wife, Garilyn, coming towards me. They were all smiles. They seemed to be feeling optimistic about the voting. I was surprised. I hadn't felt quite so optimistic, but they had noticed that there were thirty-five percent or so who voted for the resolutions. They felt that was progress from the first time I had done this in 2007 where there were only about ten percent.

They talked with me a while and reminded me of William Wilberforce, who worked for 20 years in the British Parliament to see the slave trade abolished in England. I could not have been any more blessed by their love and support. I felt that day as if I were Moses and Aaron and Hur were on either side of me holding up my arms in battle.

I was beginning to feel more revitalized by the moment. I went back outside to make some phone calls to some people who had been praying for me and for the resolutions. I called my husband, Greg, who listened to my story with interest, and blessed me with his words of encouragement. I also called my friend and prayer partner, Iris, who had been praying during the whole process. She also was uplifting to my spirit, and feeling like God was really at work.

Then, I called my former pastor, Perry Dalton, who is like Mordecai from the book of Esther to me. He has encouraged me along the way that I must do what I have to do, "For such a time as this" (Esther 4:14). It was during this phone call that I realized for sure that I would continue. Rather than hearing him discouraged and tell me that I should throw in the towel, he said, "Well, this is wonderful! This shows real signs of hope." I was thinking, "It does? The resolutions didn't pass!" He said, "You only need another 16% for them to pass!" This was because I had told him there were about 35% this time who had voted favorably, and he knew that 51% would give us the majority. When he said that, I realized how close I really was and that now was not the time to quit.

I found a new rush of joy in the days to follow. I received some very encouraging e-mails from people who had been at the conference, or had heard about what had happened. I also received a very encouraging phone call from a pastor that I did not know within the Alabama West Florida Conference, who said I should keep going, and not quit! All these things, God used to get me back to where I needed to be.

I feel a sense of God's presence and joy when I pursue what is the call on my life, to help the church understand that we must stand with Israel, and to be a blessing to the Jewish people in these last days. Most importantly, due to the ways that the Jewish people have been treated over the last few hundred years at the hands of Christians, it is now our responsibility to tear down these walls so that they can receive the love of their Messiah and be saved.

The Hidden Message at the Fall Festival

    The Lord seems to have this pattern with me when it comes to His feasts from Leviticus 23. It seems like so many times He has done something really special for me on these days when they come up on the Jewish calendar. I love when He does this kind of thing, because I don't even have to go looking for it. He just jumps in and teaches me the reality of the lesson in whatever particular feast it happens to be.

    On one particular year, it was the first day of the Feast of Tabernacles. This is where the Jewish people build temporary shelters with palm branches and live in them for a week. I was a little bummed out because I didn't have anything Jewish planned. I always like to do something to commemorate the day. I certainly don't do it because I feel that I must. I'm not under the law, but I enjoy learning what I can through celebrating the feasts in some way. I have been known to go out in my back yard and decorate under the palm tree that is wedged between our garage and fence. I enjoy sitting out there off and on throughout the week, even if it is just me.

    This time, He exceeded my best efforts with a full-blown picture of the Millennial reign of Messiah! Our friend, Dane, who was one of our young people in Bible study many years ago, called me on a Friday night. He is now married to Aimee and they have an adorable little boy. Anyway, Dane is a really awesome singer and musician. He called and asked if I wanted to play violin with him at a gig out at Pier Park, a local shopping area. I said, "Sure!" I love short notice for playing gigs. I really do, since I prefer playing interpretive violin rather than notes on paper.

Not really realizing what I had said "yes" to, I went. When I got there, I realized that this was a bigger event that I had thought. It was in a beautiful, large grassy field. There were hundreds of people there. The event was put on by a local United Methodist Church. I followed the sound of the music, and found Dane and Aimee. They were getting ready to set up under this large pavilion with a big sound system. I got my violin out and set up. I was just enjoying the experience of playing along, when Dane got to talking about a song he had written that we were about to play.

The song was called, "Behold, the Bridegroom Cometh." It was from the book of Hosea, Chapter 2. It told the story about a bride who wandered off into the wilderness, and the husband went looking for her. That is the very short version, but it was a picture of how God comes looking for us when we wander off from Him, and He does it in love. In the book of Hosea, it is actually referring to the nation of Israel. This book speaks volumes about God's plan for the nation of Israel to come home and celebrate a wedding. It says that Israel will call Him, "Husband." It is beautiful imagery and Dane's song was all about this.

As we began to play the song, I happened to look up. When I did, I was jolted into the spirit realm, able to see with spiritual eyes. I knew we were under a pavilion, but I didn't notice till then that it was shaped in a big arch, and looked like a giant palm frond!

Suddenly, I looked over the grassy field, at the hundreds of people, while Dane was singing the song from Hosea 2 about the Bridegroom coming. It was then that I realized that I was having sort of a flash forward, to the Millennial, or one thousand year reign of Christ in the future. It will be during a time when Zechariah 14:16 says that "all the nations will come up to worship the Lord at the Feast of Tabernacles." I looked out, and realized that there were many tents set up all around the perimeter of the green, grassy field. There were hundreds of people, and balloons, food, fun, and lots of activity going on, and we were up under the palm frond worshiping the Lord! I even noticed that over the tops of some of the tents, palm trees were sticking up! Of course, none of this had been planned, but it was there just the same for me to see when I saw with my spiritual eyes.

For years I had dreamed of the Methodist Church making "aliyah" in a spiritual sense. The actual meaning of the word is *to come up* and is about Jewish people immigrating to Israel. In my way of thinking, for the church, it meant *coming up higher* in their understanding of blessing Israel. I have fought some battles in trying to change the church's official Resolution 312 about Israel. I have spent much time, energy and thought into what I could do to be an agent for change. I had about decided that I was done. Maybe I had done all I could. I still didn't quite know the answer to that, but I can just say that I was very encouraged by what I saw in the Spirit that day.

At first I felt a quick sadness sweep over me, realizing that even though it was actually the time of Feast of Tabernacles, probably not too many there knew it. This was because much of our understanding about God's seasons and celebrations had been taken away from us, the church, in the days when Constantine was the Roman emperor. He had forbidden all forms of Jewish worship, and this was where much of our understanding of our Jewish roots had been lost. Maybe someone there knew it was a Jewish holiday, but that is not why they were having the celebration. It was more of a Christian Fall Fest, which was really nice. Looking at it from another perspective, I realized that this is exactly what it will be like someday, when we all come together, Jew and Gentile, as one in the Messiah.

Every year, Jewish people all over the world go up to Jerusalem for this harvest festival, and if they can't go up, they are at home, making Sukkah's, (tents, or booths). They live in them for seven days. They spend time together as families and friends, laughing, playing together, and they are thankful. They are commemorating the time when God was a shelter over them as they were wandering in the wilderness. I don't know how much the Jewish people are thinking about the Millennial Kingdom when they celebrate Sukkot, but it is talked about, as I said, in Zechariah chapter 14. It will happen in reality in the Millennial reign of Messiah, when He comes to set up His throne upon the earth.

Here we were, at the Christian fest and I looked out over this beautiful green grass and hundreds of people, playing, laughing, having fun, rejoicing, going from tent to tent, and I saw how it will be someday.

I stood there crying while I was playing, and I was having an encounter with God. To make it even sweeter, I looked and saw Amber, another of our former Bible study kids, all grown up, standing there with her little daughter Olivia, listening to us play. They smiled and waved at me, and I cried some more. It was like a reunion, which is how it will be in the Millennial Kingdom.

When we were done, I was standing there and realized I was surrounded with young people that had been part of my life in the past. There was Dane, Aimee, Amber, and also Cameron, from our former youth group. She is now the youth director at a United Methodist Church. Her sister Katie was there, who I had taught to play violin years ago. All of them were there, gathered around, and I had so much joy in my heart to be reunited with all of them and see what awesome men and women of God they had turned out to be.

Cameron's group got up to play with her United Methodist Church praise band. They were playing lots of different music, including some secular songs. God was speaking to me through this music. Trains have always been a significant part of my ministry, *East River*, starting with my friend, Sherri. She always envisioned the train as a symbol of something that had been once used for evil in Nazi Germany, taking Jews to the concentration camps, now turned in the other direction, for good. It was symbolic of, perhaps, the church, linked together in interdependence, to help the Jewish people.

When Cameron's group got up and performed the song "Love Train," it caught my attention, especially when I was sitting there listening and thought I heard the word *Israel*. Later I asked her for a copy of the music, and I just started laughing. It spelled out perfectly what I was seeing with the future "Feast of Tabernacles." Here are the words:

> People all over the world, join hands,
> start a love train - love train...
> The next stop that we make will be England,
> Tell all the folks in Russia and China too,
> Don't you know that it's time to get on board,
> and let this train keep on riding, riding on through...
> All your brothers over in Africa,
> Tell the folks in Egypt and **Israel** too,
> Please don't miss this train at your station,
> 'cause if you miss it I feel sorry, sorry for you...[9] *[my emphasis]*

I believe prophetically, for me, this was the message, that the Methodist church and many others will get it. They will be getting on board the "train," and they will be part of the restoration of Israel and the nations!

---

[9] *Love Train* performed by the O'Jays. Philadelphia International. Kenny Gamble and Leon Huff-1972

The Clue in the Mexican Sombrero

Who would have thought that a huge mystery was about to be unlocked that day while I was sitting in a Mexican restaurant? I was with my new friend, Esther, who was a native-born Navajo Indian. She loved Mexican food and that particular Mexican restaurant. We were getting to know each other after we had formed an instant friendship based on some amazing circumstances.

We had originally met during a women's breakfast. We began discussing our lives, and eventually, I told her about my ministry, *East River*. When I told her of my interest in helping the Jews make aliyah, (immigrate to Israel), she was blown away.

It turned out that for some unknown reason, for years, she had been saving newspaper clippings of Jewish people making aliyah. She had a file-folder full of them. Esther was in the United States Air Force, and since the Air Force had actually helped in bringing some of these Jewish people back to Israel, she had become very interested. This, however, was really the only thing she knew about Israel and the Jewish people. It was just something she was drawn to.

That particular day, as we were in the Mexican restaurant, I felt an anticipation that God was up to something. She had told me that she was raised on the West Coast in a Mexican-Navajo family who had roots from Mexico and became Christians. Her father was an Assembly of God evangelist, and her family sang gospel music. In more recent years, her father had developed an interest in Jewish things for reasons that he did not understand. He just knew he had a desire to purchase a tallit (Jewish prayer shawl) and was visiting a synagogue.

A few years before, I had become aware that many Hispanic people had hidden Jewish genealogy, and I was now curious about Esther. That day I brought a book with me by Dr. Dell Sanchez that listed the surnames of many hidden Jewish people of Spanish heritage.[10]

As we sat and visited, I asked what her maiden name was, as well as her mother's maiden name. I looked them up in the book, and to our amazement, both names were there! In that moment, a whole new realm was opened up to Esther, which was the strong possibility that somewhere in her background were some hidden Sephardic (Hispanic) Jews; hidden to protect themselves from the fiery trials of the Spanish and Portuguese Inquisitions. Now we understood why Esther and her father were being drawn to the things that were Jewish. It was in their DNA.

A while after this lunch with Esther, I was with my mother-in-law in the Historic St. Andrew District of Panama City, just shopping and spending some time with her. We went into a little consignment and second-hand clothing shop and were looking around. We were about to leave when I noticed a Mexican sombrero up on the shelf. I knew immediately that was what it was but had never seen a real one, or if I ever had, did not remember. What got my attention was the very colorful Magen David (Star of David) design that was embroidered onto it.

I went over to look at it and explained to my mother-in-law that I liked it because I had learned about the modern-day Sephardic Jews who were making aliyah (immigrating to Israel). They were coming from different places in the world, as they were uncovering their formerly hidden Sephardic destiny as spoken of in Obadiah 1:20.

And the exiles of this host of the sons of Israel,
Who are among the Canaanites as far as Zarephath,

---

10 Dr. Dell Sanchez, *Aliyah! The Exodus Continues*, Authors Choice Press, 2001, 2006 Authors Choice Press.
http://www.4sephardim.com/project.html

Operation Olive Branch

And the exiles of Jerusalem who are in Sepharad
Will possess the cities of the Negev.

They were dispersed all over the world during the Babylonian, Assyrian and various conquests. They are part of what is called the "Diaspora," along with other Jews, like Ashkenazi, who went to other parts of the world at various times throughout history. The Jewish people are now returning to the land of Israel from many places. The Sephardim in particular, are returning to the Negev Desert in fulfillment of this ancient Bible prophecy of Obadiah. The Negev is their inheritance.

The Sephardic Jews originally went to Spain, which was also known as Sepharad or the Iberian Peninsula. During the Spanish Inquisition, amidst much persecution, they were forced to convert or be killed. They were finally expelled from Spain in 1492, and sent to South America and North America, beginning with Columbus, who, by the way, many believe was a Jewish believer in Yeshua/Jesus.

The 9th of Av on the Hebrew calendar was the day both Jewish temples had been destroyed in times past. August 3, 1492 was the 9th of Av, the day Columbus set sail, hoping to reach India by sailing west. He had Jews and Christians sailing with him.

Naturally, some Jewish people wound up in Mexico, so, when I saw the sombrero with the Star of David, I felt this was a confirmation to the above facts. I didn't buy it that day, but later did go back and buy it as a gift for Esther.

Not long after that, I was having one of those days where I felt a little displaced, like maybe I was out in a spiritual "Diaspora" somewhere, wandering around, doubting all of the promises God had made to me concerning my life and ministry. I guess this happens sometimes to anyone who senses a call from God in some form or another. Anyway, the rain from a tropical storm was coming down, so I stayed in my house, and was feeling a little weepy.

About 9 p.m. that night, God did one of his surprises that He does sometimes to encourage me. I received a newsletter from Dell

Sanchez and the Sephardic Anusim Center in the Negev. This is where they are absorbing all the Sephardic Jews that are coming in. I began to read his newsletter, when God grabbed me. It was titled, "Operation Serape!"

It explained that another group of Jewish people were expected to make aliyah to the Negev soon. He noted that these were not from South America or a Latin American country or island, but that this group of Anusim of Hispanic background were 4th and 5th generation citizens of the United States!

They had previously thought they were Gentiles (Goyim) but have recently discovered through "genealogies, history and now through DNA that they're bona fide descendants of Spanish Jews."

The article told how in 1949-1950, forty-nine thousand Yemeni Jews were airlifted to Israel because of anti-Semitism. This was right after Israel became a nation again in 1948. The project was called "Operation Magic Carpet." The comparison was being made that the new Hispanic Sephardic aliyah could similarly be called "Operation Serape." The newsletter explained that the "serape was used as a secret prayer shawl" (a Jewish tallit).

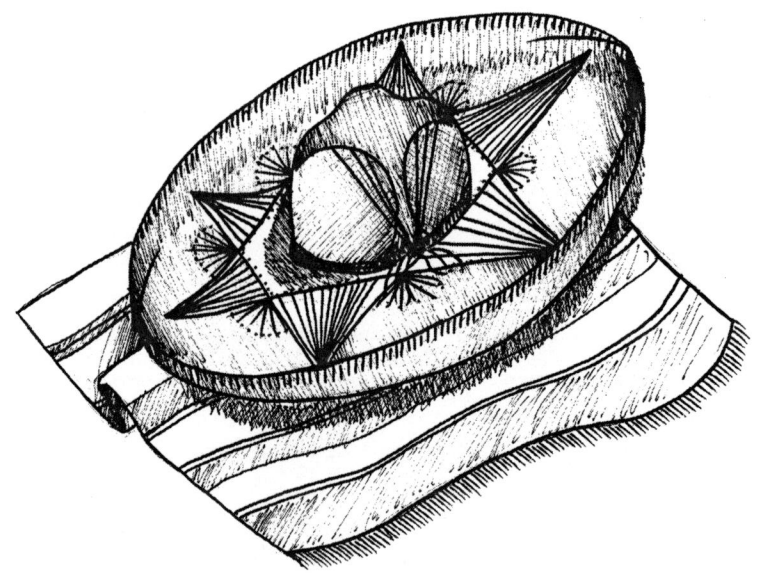

What Dell Sanchez said next blew me away! He said, "The next time you get a chance, check the *top of a Mexican Sombrero*. Chances are that you'll find a *Star of David* [woven] on the top of it." I was shocked and extremely blessed to read this! I was thanking the Lord for His faithfulness to me that day when I was feeling down about my calling. He re-affirmed me, His daughter, and helped me to see a bigger picture through the use of a beautiful Mexican/Jewish sombrero.

After I gave Esther the sombrero, she remembered that in an old family trunk, she already had not only her own Mexican sombrero with a Star of David, but her own Mexican Serape as well! Of course, she didn't know there was anything Jewish about them when her parents gave them to her. To Esther, it was about her Mexican/Navajo Indian heritage. However, as previously mentioned, we now knew that she had two Jewish last names in her family, her Mom's maiden name, as well as her Dad's name. God is doing a work here that we can't even begin to fathom!

More recently, Esther's father came to live with her before he died. She had a beautiful moment with him when she asked him to put his Jewish tallit on and pray for her, his oldest daughter. She said it was a moment she would never forget. Esther and her father are examples of many hidden Sephardic Jews who are coming to understand their identity, not only as part of the Jewish race, but also their identity in the Jewish and Gentile Messiah of the world, Yeshua (Jesus).

God's Mysterious Connections

I love the way God works. If your heart is for Him, and your thoughts are toward His will and purpose in your life, then it truly is like living a great adventure! You never know what each day will bring.

Sometimes, you just feel like you are going through the motions of life, and wondering when the exciting part is really going to kick in, but it's in the day-in, day-out experiences that God shapes us, molds us and puts us on track with His plans. You really can't mess up too badly if you belong to Him, and you trust Him to lead you where He wants you to go, because He takes even our mistakes and works them together for good.

One of the first really cool connections God made for me was quite a few years ago. I must mention here my friend, Richard Ward, a "Messianic Gentile" (a Gentile Christian who loves all things Jewish and is into the Jewish roots of his faith). I had heard of a Jewish dance group at a local church in Pensacola and had gone over to see them dance. I was just taken in with the joy of these people dancing these Jewish dances to the Lord! I soon joined the group and danced with them for many years.

With them, I learned many things about Jewish music, culture, and even learned some Hebrew through the words to the songs. This was an awesome time in my life. I had much happiness, as on Saturday mornings and Tuesday evenings, I would take my three boys up to Charity Chapel, and they would run around and play in the big fellowship hall while I was learning to dance for the Lord. This was something that shaped the future of who I would become, as a lover of the God of Israel, and of His people.

Richard stayed faithful over many, many years to teach more and more people how to do this beautiful form of worship. He and his brothers and parents constantly choreographed new dances for us. Later in life, he even learned to speak and read Hebrew, and he and his wife, Ruth, came and taught some classes through *East River Ministries* in Panama City. Richard is also a wonderful Messianic singer and guitar player, and we have had many opportunities in later years to play Messianic praise and worship together. I thank God for these faithful servants.

On another occasion many years later, I was sitting at my desk at the United Methodist Church where I worked, and the associate minister came into my office and invited me to be a part of a meeting he was going to have shortly with a particular couple who had an appointment. I was a little surprised that he asked me to do this, since my duties involved mostly office work.

When he told me what the subject matter was, I knew why he had asked. This was a Messianic Jewish couple, believers in Yeshua/Jesus the Messiah. He knew I had a love and interest in all things Jewish, so he felt led to invite me. I thank God for people who listen to the Lord's leading and are obedient to it.

Michael and Mimi met with us in the library. They told us their story, of how they, as Jewish people, had come to a personal relationship with God through Jesus. They were actually members of Frazier United Methodist Church in Montgomery, the same place where the Alabama West Florida Annual Conference is held every year.

M & M, as I would eventually call them, had been called to missions to begin a Jewish outreach in South Florida. They were trying to get churches involved in supporting them so that they could move to this area that was home to many American Jews. The Jewish community of South Florida is the 5th largest Jewish population in the country!

This began my involvement and friendship with this wonderful couple that continues to this day. They traveled around Alabama and the Gulf Coast of Florida, gaining support until finally, they were able to fulfill their dream and move south. They named their ministry, *Everlasting Life Outreach*.

One day, they came over to Panama City, Florida to meet my pastor and his wife, and to visit the *East River Ministries* office upstairs. We had an absolutely wonderful time of fellowship and enjoying God's presence together. We prayed, and God really connected our hearts in love for each other, because we shared a common vision for the salvation of the Jewish people.

The work that they do in South Florida is so significant. They live in a condominium complex that is nothing but Jewish people who need salvation. They post invitations to Bible studies on the community bulletin board, and are always looking for ways to share the love of Jesus with their Jewish friends. Who would understand this better than two Jewish people who have found the love of their Messiah? And they are being rewarded for their labor, because Jewish people do accept their invitations for Bible study and fellowship, and some are coming to know their Messiah Yeshua.

Michael and Mimi have hosted two dialogues on the subject of whether or not Jesus is the Jewish Messiah. The dialogues were between two different Jewish Rabbis in South Florida, and Dr. Michael Brown, who is a believing Jewish scholar. Hundreds of the Jewish community came out for these events. Michael and Mimi are always looking for creative ways to bring the gospel to the Jewish people.

Another Jewish believer that I met in Israel is Brian Slater, who is originally from California. He lives In Israel with his wife, Racheli, who is a native-born Israeli, and their three children. They are an incredible family who have given their lives to live in Israel and reach out to the hurting and homeless, drug addicts, prostitutes and alcoholics with God's love. Brian works through *Chosen People Ministries* and manages three soup kitchens and a free medical clinic in Israel. Anyone who needs help can come there, whether they are Jewish, Palestinian or Christian, and receive love and help.

One of the most fun things I have been able to do in ministry was to host Brian in Florida. He came over from Israel, and various groups were organized for him to speak and raise support. He stayed in a little apartment at Laguna Beach Christian Retreat, and for a week this was his home-base to reach out and make new friends who would wind up being a blessing to Israel through his ministry.

My job that week was to make the contacts for him, and to help people to know what he does over in Israel in his outreach. I felt inspired to decorate his room at Laguna Beach with an Israel flag, and other assorted Jewish items, and to have some Jewish worship music playing. The Lord led me in these preparations, as I thought of the hard work that he does in Israel, always being on the go in ministry. It made my heart full of joy to see the delight and sense of being refreshed that he had in his place to seek God during that week.

There have been times God has blessed requests for money for different ministries. Once, Brian needed a car badly to be able to do his ministry in picking up and delivering food for the soup kitchen. It just so happened that my son needed a car as well. Brian's car kept breaking down, and in my son's car, water was actually filling up his floorboards. None of us had any money, Brian for his car or us for ours. Before I realized how much my son needed a new car, I had become aware of Brian's need, so I did the only thing I could do, which was send out an e-mail, explaining his situation and asking for help.

Overnight, there were seven-hundred dollars in pledges for Brian's car! The next day, when my son presented his problem to me, and I knew we didn't have any money, I felt that we should ask God in faith for it. I did not send out an e-mail request for our car situation. However, overnight Nick had the answer to his prayer and his car problem was solved! He was driving a nice truck before the week was out. I have to wonder if that was because we met the needs of one of God's chosen people first. I don't know, but it was interesting timing on everything. God does say that if we bless His chosen people, we will be blessed!

Many times I have not had money to do things, but God has shown me creative ways I could use whatever gifts He has given me. I happen to enjoy writing and making blogs, and God has used me a couple of times with the two ministries that I mentioned to make these blogs for them so that they could have a place to post newsletters and pictures. It is a small thing to me to make these blogs, but I think it was helpful to them. It also connected me more personally with these ministries, as I am now in closer contact with what they are doing.

All of these things matter in the Kingdom. I tell you these stories, hopefully, to inspire you to reach out in whatever ways God brings across your path to be a blessing to Israel and the Jewish people. Each little thing we do in His name has a ripple effect for the Kingdom.

One of the nights Brian was here, we had a gathering at a place called The Rabbit Hole. We called it "Israeli Night," and many people who love Israel from our city came. We rejoiced with Jewish dancing and music and Israeli food, while Brian shared about his ministry in Israel.

I, being a Gentile Christian, have the utmost respect for all of these people and what they are about. *East River* has tried in various ways to support them. We haven't had large sums of money to give them, although I pray constantly for more money to help them.

Another area we have felt it is important to focus is in blessing Jewish people and Israel, even the ones who do not believe in Yeshua as Messiah. Why do we do this? It is because of all the persecution and rejection the Jewish people have endured over hundreds of years, by Christians. There is a wall between us, because we have called them "Christ killers," and have had anti-Semitic thoughts and deeds toward them. Even if we have not done these things personally, sometimes we just esteem them lightly, and even that is wrong. They are God's chosen people. We need to let them know that we are different, and that we truly love them unconditionally.

One of the most memorable things that happened very early in this ministry was a "Night to Honor Israel" at our church. It came about in an unusual way. I was with some friends over at the local Reform Temple to celebrate Hanukkah and to show our love and support for the Jewish people there. Afterward, we were knoshing (eating and mingling) with the Rabbi. He was an older gentleman, very kind and welcoming to us Christians. He never questioned why we were there, but invited us in.

I asked him, "So, Rabbi, how many times have you been to Israel?" I just assumed he had been there at least a couple of times in his life. He was about 72 years old at the time. He really surprised me when he said, "Never."

I said, "Really? Never? Why not?"

Then he told me the story of how he had worked in sales for many years before feeling like it was his calling in life to start a synagogue. The congregation had begun meeting in a library of a school, and then in a church, and finally, they had worked enough to be able to build an actual building. He had then gone to a Rabbinic school in Chicago and had gotten his certification to lead the congregation. He had never had the time, money or resources to take such a trip.

I left there feeling a stirring in my spirit. The very next morning, I woke up, and just had a very strong impression that we must find a way to get him and his wife to Israel. Then a friend who had been part of that conversation the night before, called and said exactly the same thing. I knew this was what we must do. That particular friend, Linda, actually donated the first one-thousand dollars toward the trip.

I made a poster for the campaign that I put out at the church. It had a picture of Florida and a big ocean and Israel on the other side. There was a little rabbi, flying across the ocean on a plane. As more and more money came in, he would get closer and closer to Israel. It was a really fun project for the whole church.

The time came when we had made five-thousand dollars, and we knew it was enough to get them a trip to Israel, but we didn't want to just go and hand them a check. We wanted it to be special, so we decided to have a "Night to Honor Israel," and invite their congregation over. I didn't know if they would accept, but they did, not knowing about the money.

It was an incredible feeling to see three rows of precious Jewish people, sitting up front that night. We had Jewish music playing, and dancers and worshipers who did some beautifully choreographed songs with meaningful words. Also, as it turned out, when some members of our congregation got up to do a Jewish dancethe Jewish people got up and danced too! We all danced in a circle, together, and it was incredible! It was a picture of how it will be someday, as we all dance together in the Kingdom, as one in the Messiah.

We tried to be sensitive as we did not want them to feel like we were trying to bring them in and beat them over the head with a Bible. We simply wanted to show them extravagant love. Billy Morgan did a wonderful job as the Master of Ceremonies that night, sharing pertinent scriptures from the Torah that we could all enjoy. We had a wonderful spread of Israeli-type foods that our church people brought.

Then the moment came when we presented the check to them. We told them that it was a no strings attached gift of love. Everyone cried that night. The Rabbi's wife said, "I had just told my husband that I thought we would never get to go to Israel!" As it turned out, they spent their 52nd wedding anniversary in Jerusalem. He prayed at the Wailing Wall wearing a new Tallit (prayer shawl) his wife bought for him in a Jerusalem gift shop.

We formed a bond of love with those people that, at least in my heart, will never be broken. It was an amazing "God opportunity" and we continue to pray for those people, that they would always remember and know the love of God. We pray that someday they will receive their Jewish Messiah.

I have another Jewish friend, Eliezer, who travels around from country to country, raising support for the brave pioneers and settlers of Samaria, which is the Biblical term for what is known as the modern day West Bank.

I was asked by my friend, Deborah Kellogg, if I would host him for a few days and find speaking engagements for him, which I did. Although he does not share the same beliefs as I do in Jesus, we found that we had many things in common in our faith. After all, the Jewish nation of Israel is the rich root from which we Christians came. Jesus was, in fact, a Jewish man, raised in a Jewish home, and all the early disciples were Jewish!

This man puts his life on the line every day to live in Israel, after making aliyah, (immigrating) to Israel in the '80s. His whole family are observant Jews, and they have built their life in Israel, knowing that every day they are in danger. They sense instinctively that they must do what they are doing. They felt they had to go there and live, and work and grow. Eliezer helps other immigrants to do the same by raising funds to build their communities in an area where even our government wants them to stop building. They continue, even at the risk of their lives, because they believe that it is their heritage and destiny to do so.

When Eliezer came to Florida, we spent a week getting to know him and a strong friendship of love and support was formed. He understands that we have our differences and yet, we accept each other as we are. Do I hope and pray that he will receive the Messiah Yeshua? Yes. Of course! But I cannot make him, nor change him. I respect God's work in and around Him, and trust that God's ways are not our ways.

He does realize that Christians are the best friends that the Jewish people have. This did not come easy. He had to work through a lot of forgiveness and overlooking how his people have been treated by Christians, but the rewards of the friendship have now outweighed the difficulties. God is doing a work in Christians these days, opening their eyes to how we have treated the Jewish people, and we are repenting and asking forgiveness of the Jewish people. This has to happen in order for restoration to occur.

Cynthia Hillson has also influenced my life. I met her at a conference at *Christian International* in Santa Rosa Beach, Florida several years ago, and was touched by her ministry, *Precious Oils Up On the Hill*. She travels to Israel several times a year, bringing gifts and humanitarian aid to the Jewish people. She takes donations of toys, clothing, medical supplies and other items, "schlepping" them from North Carolina to Israel and back. She goes into hospitals, and into the streets of Jerusalem and other places, and gives out these gifts of love from Christians to Jewish people, and whomever God wants.

She also is creative in her ways of raising funds for herself to travel. She is an apothecary, bringing herbs and plants from Israel, and mixing them to make anointing oils, each with a little story. That is one of her many gifts.

I have been so blessed to have family, friends, a pastor and his wife, and a church family that is so supportive of what *East River* does. Many times, I have called on them and the volunteers have been there! They provide everything from dance, to decorations for tables, to food, to music! I can't list all of them, but it is amazing to see the Body of Messiah come together for a common purpose.

There are many more people who have ministries like these that I could mention here, but I cannot list them all. These are only some of the divine connections that God has brought across my path, and I know there will be many more, as I continue on this great adventure, uncovering mystery after mystery!

The Twelve Tribes Mystery

I was spending time one September day with my mom in Pensacola. We were sitting together watching some morning programming on television. Just prior to that, my mind had been consumed with wondering what I was supposed to do next with *East River*. I had been thinking about fundraising and how I might go about it. I was envisioning a big banquet with people coming and donating lots of money to bless Israel through *East River Ministries*. What began as an idea for fundraising turned into so much more; something that was deep and rich and meaningful.

As I sat there with Mom, my mind was on these things and I wasn't too focused on the TV program. However, one of the stories we were listening to caught my attention. Some people were going to begin hosting dinner parties to help raise funds for hunger in America. Suddenly, my imagination was off and running. I had an idea! We could have dinner parties too! I picked up a pencil and paper to take some notes. For whatever reason, I wrote the number 12. I looked at it and then wrote down 12 x 12 = 144. We started playing with math and then figured that it would take one thousand people giving $12 per month to give us a budget of $144,000 per year.

Mom and I continued to discuss where I might be headed with my little math equations (*and* my ministry!). She started giving me her thoughts and reminded me that the number 144,000 is in the book of Revelation somewhere. I said, "Yes, you are right!" I got my Bible out and looked it up. Revelation 7:4-8 says,

> *And I heard the number of those who were sealed, one hundred and forty-four thousand sealed from every tribe of the sons of*

Israel; from the tribe of Judah, twelve thousand were sealed, from the tribe of Reuben twelve thousand, from the tribe of Gad twelve thousand, from the tribe of Asher twelve thousand, from the tribe of Naphtali twelve thousand, from the tribe of Manasseh twelve thousand, from the tribe of Simeon twelve thousand, from the tribe of Levi twelve thousand, from the tribe of Issachar twelve thousand, from the tribe of Zebulun twelve thousand, from the tribe of Joseph twelve thousand, from the tribe of Benjamin, twelve thousand were sealed.

The idea of the dinner parties, however, was the really great part of what came out of all our talking and dreaming that day. Our focus began to shift to how the number twelve represented the twelve tribes of Israel in a more literal sense. We knew that in the Scriptures, there was promised a restoration of the nation of Israel. Since the motto of *East River Ministries* is "Restoring the Land and the People to Israel," this concept peaked my interest.

Although we knew that there were varying ideas on the eschatology of the Revelation 7 passage, we felt that this certainly agreed with what we understood in the context of Scripture - that God is doing a literal restoration of the people to the land of Israel, as they are beginning to come from all over the world. Immediately after the one hundred forty-four thousand are presented in that passage, Revelation 7:9 says,

After these things I looked, and behold, a great multitude which no one could count, from every nation and all tribes and peoples and tongues, standing before the throne and before the Lamb, clothed in white robes, and palm branches were in their hands...

In Revelation 14:4, it says that they are purchased as "firstfruits" to God and to the Lamb. The one hundred and forty-four thousand from the twelve tribes of Israel were apparently going to be witnesses during the tribulation period. It seemed they would, in some way, play a part in many multitudes of people being saved.

We knew that the tribes of Israel had been scattered all over the world, but as God had promised, were now being brought back and restored to their land. We talked about how it looked as if God was orchestrating events leading toward His ultimate plans. Putting all these Scriptures, thoughts and understandings together, a more concrete idea began to form.

What if, at the dinner parties, we began to pray for this restoration? We could see according to the Word of God that it would happen, so we felt it would be in line with God's will to pray for this.

We wondered where these tribes had gone. Ten of them were considered "lost," and yet, God knows exactly where they are. My mother and I continued to look through the scriptures that day, reading the original story of Jacob, whose name God changed to Israel, the father of twelve sons. These twelve sons became the nation of Israel. God had promised them the land of Canaan over and over throughout their history. It was promised to them as an everlasting covenant. Psalm 105:6-15 sums up these promises:

O seed of Abraham, His servant, O sons of Jacob, His chosen ones! He is the LORD our God; His judgments are in all the earth. He has remembered His covenant forever, the word which He commanded to a thousand generations. The covenant which He made with Abraham, and His oath to Isaac. Then He confirmed it to Jacob for a statute, to Israel as an everlasting covenant, saying, **"To you I will give the land of Canaan as the portion of your inheritance,"** *when they were only a few men in number, very few, and strangers in it. And they wandered about from nation to nation, from one kingdom to another people. He permitted no man to oppress them, and He reproved kings for their sakes; 'Do not touch My anointed ones, and do My prophets no harm.(my emphasis)*

Mom and I were on a "spiritual high" as we discussed the reality of what this meant in the day we live in. The idea for the "Twelve Tribes Small Groups" was birthed that day. A plan was quickly put into place to find twelve leaders who would open their homes once a month for dinner parties. Fundraising became the lesser emphasis, realizing that this was an incredible opportunity to gather support for the nation of Israel through prayer. People usually enjoy gathering in small groups to eat (at least that has been my experience). If, during these dinner groups, some basic understanding and prayer for Israel could happen, this would fulfill the heart of my mission.

We talked about each of the twelve groups being called by the name of one of the twelve tribes. One would be "Reuben," another "Simeon," another, "Levi," etc. Within those twelve groups, there would be, hopefully, at least twelve people gathering monthly. Each month, they would have a discussion on each of the twelve tribes and would focus their prayers that night on that one particular tribe. By the end of the year, they would have covered all twelve.

It was only after coming to all these realizations and ideas that I thought about what day it was. The date was September 15, 2009. This was the five-year anniversary of my friend Sherri's death. I usually always remembered the date of her death, but that particular day, I had completely forgotten about it; that is, until after this vision for the Twelve Tribes Small Groups unfolded. When I realized what day it was, I felt this was confirmation that this was indeed part of what God had called me to do. (For more understanding on how this all relates, and how profound it was to me, the chapter entitled, "The Mysterious Wild-Eyed Woman" will give further insight.)

I soon began formulating the plans for the tribes. I wrote up a description of how the groups would operate, and began sending it out to potential leaders. People began to get excited and give input. Our pastor's wife, Garilyn, drew a beautiful set of posters with the symbols for the twelve tribes, which we used in different ways. We had a party at our church to launch not only the Twelve Tribes Small Groups, but also, what I called the "$144,000 Campaign." They turned out to be two different ideas, related somewhat, but operating independently.

Over the course of the year, the various groups would meet. Month by month, I would sit down with the Lord and begin researching each tribe. I would write a discussion guide that consisted of several pages of information, from the beginnings of that particular tribe, which was the birth of the twelve sons to Jacob and his wives.

Also included were other interesting facts; for example, where the tribes camped around the tabernacle when they were wandering in the wilderness, i.e., north, south, east or west. Research also uncovered the particular stone that represented each tribe, which was part of the ephod of the High Priest. He wore this breastplate when He went into the Holy of Holies, taking the names of the sons of Israel before God.

Each month's discussion guide also included geographical information as to where the tribes settled in the land of Israel, and how it related to Old and New Testament stories. It also included information on where they might have gone over the last two to three thousand years, and finally, where they might wind up as they are restored to the land. All this information was taken from the Bible and Biblically-related sources.

When the year ended, the curriculum was completed and stored in my computer, ready to be used for future groups.

A Hanukkah party was planned for December with the tribes coming together to celebrate the wonderful things that had happened that year. The room was decorated with the theme of the twelve tribes. Even the decorating process turned into an educational and fun "scavenger hunt" type activity, as we searched for an item to represent each of the tribes for a centerpiece. A table was set up to fry potato latkes, a traditional Jewish Hanukkah dish. The tables were arranged in the order of the tribes as they were camped in the wilderness.

That night we had a very special guest speaker, Cynthia Hillson. Cynthia travels in and out of Israel and takes humanitarian aid, and fulfills various "God-assignments." One of those recent assignments had been to return a set of flags of the twelve tribes to Timna Park in the Arabah Valley region of the Negev. There is a full-size replica there of the Biblical tabernacle of Moses. Cynthia told us the amazing story of how she had been asked to be the caretaker of these flags, helping them to find their place back at the tabernacle.

A woman had approached her earlier that year while she was at the Feast of Tabernacles in Jerusalem, a celebration that takes place every year, hosted by the International Christian Zionist Center. During this week-long gathering, people come to Jerusalem from all over the world; a visual picture of the tribes of Israel who will come up someday to the Millennial tabernacle where Yeshua (Jesus) will rule and reign (Zechariah 14:16). Knowing of Cynthia's frequent travels throughout Israel, the woman asked Cynthia if she might possibly be able to return these flags to their new home at the tabernacle exhibit at Timna Park.

In what turned out to be a divine series of circumstances, Cynthia said, "Yes." The flags were contained in a special case called a Pro-Bazooka. Her explanation at our party of the definition of regular bazooka, a portable, tubular rocket launcher, brought a few chuckles. These flags had been used for a different kind of warfare, a spiritual one, as they had been waved as a praise offering before the Lord for two years at the Feast of Tabernacles. It made for an interesting story and word picture, to say the least.

Cynthia was not able to return the flags on that same trip but wound up going right back to Israel three weeks later on a mission to return the flags. She was also delivering some jewelry supplies on the same trip to some believers for their business. Within the jewelry supplies were hundreds of gemstones. She felt that a representation of the gemstones of the tribes should be included with the delivery of the flags. After unpacking the flags, she placed three stones in each of the four directions as part of her prayers for the restoration of the twelve tribes to modern-day Israel.

This whole incident so mirrored what we had been praying and studying with our Twelve Tribes Small groups, that when I asked her if she would come and be our guest speaker at the end of the year Hanukkah party, she readily said, "Yes!" She had been anxiously awaiting someone to tell the story to. There was turning out to be much more to this story than I even realized!

She told us the night after she had returned home from delivering the flags, thinking her mission was done, she was surprised to receive an e-mail from two Dutch women that she knew from the Feast of Tabernacles celebration. They had heard about her story of taking the flags to the Tabernacle from a mutual friend, Deborah Kellogg, whose ministry includes a prayer house in Arad in the Negev.

Incidentally, Deborah Kellogg happened to be the woman who led the tour to Israel that I had taken in 2007. That alone, I felt, was an interesting enough "coincidence"; but there was still more.

The two Dutch women had been contacted by some friends of theirs in the Netherlands. They also had a set of Twelve Tribes

flags. Now there were two sets of flags. The second set of tribe flags had been taken to many nations (used for prayer for the return of the twelve tribes) but had never been to Israel.

Within a week of Cynthia returning the flags, an incredible gathering occurred with the people who brought both sets together at the Tabernacle in the Wilderness. The flags from the Netherlands were brought to Israel and were *united* with the other set that Cynthia had placed there previously. Everyone noticed that there was a striking coordination of the two sets, although they had been constructed in two different places. One set was with long, solid colors with the names of the Tribes in English and Hebrew. The other set was silky and rectangular with the symbol of each tribe applied along with their names; also English and Hebrew. As they were draped over each other like a curtain, everyone was amazed. Even the colors coordinated.

The prayer warriors prayed into the early evening for the uniting and restoring of the twelve tribes of Israel. A few days later they met with Deborah in Arad. Here they had a prayer meeting and from there, the flags were taken to Jerusalem, to the City of David. It was Shabbat, the Jewish Sabbath, and the flags were displayed on a watchtower lookout point there. A very prominent Rabbi in the City of David happened to be passing by on his way to the Western Wall to say Shabbat prayers and was wearing his tallit. He gave the prayer warriors his blessing and smiled in agreement as they worshiped and prayed from this strategic lookout point that faces all directions; north, south, east and west. In their prayers, they called the children of Israel home, and this they did as Shabbat ended and a new day began.

It was an amazing story that Cynthia shared with us that night at the Hanukkah party. Something very significant that seemed to be highlighted with the two sets of flags was the scripture in Ezekiel 37:15-23, which reads:

> *The word of the LORD came again to me saying, "And you, son of man, take for yourself one stick and write on it, 'For* **Judah** *and for the sons of Israel, his companions'; then take another stick and write on it, 'For Joseph, the stick of* **Ephraim** *and all the*

house of Israel, his companions.' Then join them for yourself one to another into one stick, that they may become one in your hand. And when the sons of your people speak to you saying, 'Will you not declare to us what you mean by these?' say to them, 'Thus says the Lord God, "Behold, I will take the stick of Joseph, which is in the hand of Ephraim, and the tribes of Israel, his companions; and I will put them with it, with the stick of Judah, and make them one stick, and **they will be one in My hand,"'** *And the sticks on which you write will be in your hand before their eyes. And say to them, 'Thus says the Lord God,* **"Behold, I will take the sons of Israel from among the nations where they have gone, and I will gather them from every side and bring them into their own land; and I will make them one nation in the land, on the mountains of Israel** *and one king will be king for all of them; and they will no longer be two nations, and they will no longer be divided into two kingdoms. And they will no longer defile themselves with their idols, or with their detestable things, or with any of their transgressions, but I will deliver them from all their dwelling places in which they have sinned, and will cleanse them. And they will be My people and I will be their God."'* (my emphasis)

These verses speak about the restoration of the twelve tribes from all the nations of the world as they are brought back into their own land and showing without a doubt that this is the direction that we are to pray. Can it be that the prayers that have been prayed in the Twelve Tribes Small Groups have been a spiritual part of the two sets of flags coming together? If so, could the ultimate result of these prayers, and the many prayers of others around the world, be that the actual twelve tribes of Israel are being restored to their land and to their Messiah?

The most recent thing that has happened is Cynthia sent me a small packet of the twelve tribes' stones, which came from the hundreds of gemstones that she had taken to Israel. I am already using them as a point of reference for a prayer focus as I continue to pray for Israel's restoration. They remind me to pray against replacement theology wherever it may be found inside the church. This is the thinking that the church has replaced Israel, and that God is finished with them. These verses in Ezekiel and other passages completely counter-act that way of thinking, as well as the stones visually representing the twelve *literal* tribes of Israel.

I hope and pray that the Twelve Tribes Small Groups will continue happening anywhere in the world that there are people who would like to pray for Israel with a focus on restoration. The curriculum/discussion guide for all twelve tribes is now written and can be duplicated wherever there are willing hearts who will pray. In the appendix of this book is the description of how to operate a Twelve Tribes Small Group, and the vision. In Psalm 122:1-9, we as Christians have our instructions on how to pray:

> *I was glad when they said to me, 'Let us go to the house of the LORD.' Our feet are standing within your gates, O Jerusalem. Jerusalem, that is built as a city that is compact together;* **to which the tribes go up, even the tribes of the LORD, an ordinance for Israel – to give thanks to the name of the LORD.** *For there thrones were set for judgment. The thrones of the house of David.* **Pray for the peace of Jerusalem;** *May they prosper who love you; May peace be within your walls, and prosperity within your palaces. For the sake of my brothers and my friends, I will now say, 'May peace be within you.' For the sake of the house of the LORD our God, I will seek your good. [my emphasis]*

It absolutely astounds me when I think of the incredible, mysterious ways God works, dropping clues to lead us. If we are seeking His will and His ways, especially concerning His bigger picture, He will lead us into places of incredible joy! When I was sitting there with my sweet little mom that day, discussing the number 144,000, and Jacob's twelve sons, I could not have known the magnitude of what God would do! The truth is, I don't believe we have yet seen the full implications of the ripple effect of that day in September.

Sherri's Secret Message

My friend Sherri, the one who had such a passion and a love for God's chosen people, Israel, saw my brother David for the first time at my Dad's funeral. She spotted him across the room and made a bee-line for him. Her first, and only words to him, as she locked her fiery blue eyes onto his, were, **"You know you're a part of this, don't you?"** He looked at her and didn't have a clue what she was talking about.

David had recently planned his first trip to Israel to teach at a violin school there, and I had told Sherri about it; however, he did not *know* that I had told her, and was quite taken aback by this strange woman's proclamation! He didn't even know who she was, nor did he know what the "this" was of which he was a "part." He asked me later, "Who in the *world* was that strange woman at Dad's funeral who said I was a part of something, although I don't know what?" It would become more and more evident over time, however, that he indeed *was* and *is* "a part of this."

This is the way it was with many people that Sherri encountered. What she said to David, was something that she also said to other people as God would show her various things about their gifts, talents or resources. She saw many people as being part of the bigger picture of what God was doing concerning the church and Israel. This was really about the return of Yeshua/Jesus the Messiah to the Jews and to the nations. There was much work to be done in the Kingdom, and she saw many people as laborers in the harvest. I can honestly say that she was one who constantly beseeched the Lord of the Harvest to bring forth laborers (Matthew 9:38).

There have been many times I've heard her say that same phrase to people. Some got it immediately, and others, it has taken longer. Over time, it seems like those whom Sherri's life touched have come to an understanding of Israel's restoration in some quite profound ways. Her life was a ripple.

One of the main people that I know who was affected by Sherri's life was our pastor, Perry Dalton. He had been our pastor at Pine Forest United Methodist Church in Pensacola, as well as Springfield United Methodist Church in Panama City, Florida. She spent many hours excitedly sharing with him the deep revelations she was getting about Israel and the Jewish people. He, in turn, spent many hours mentoring her as she was an Asbury Seminary student. He also encouraged her in her own gifts and callings and taught her many things about ministry. Although he was skeptical in the beginning about the Israel subject, over time, he began to see it. He had some very profound moments with God revealing these truths to him.

I will never forget the day of November 22, 2003, when we were having the "In The Shadow of His Presence" conference at Springfield. We were worshiping in the sanctuary and you could really sense that the Lord was right there with us. I remember being part of that worship experience, led by our Music Minister, Alan Mullikin. I was playing my violin and we were all really caught up in that beautiful moment, knowing that the Lord was doing something special.

Sherri was a very spiritual person, with a very deep capacity to feel and love God and others. Suddenly, she got up and went over to our pastor as he was standing there with his hands lifted in the air to God. She had a Jewish prayer shawl that was very meaningful to her, and she asked if she could place it over his shoulders.

She then began to say things about his call to be an apostolic leader within the Methodist Church and also with Israel. She was praying for him that this day would always be significant, and it would be like the day that the "shot was heard around the world." I found out later that she was referring to the way the assassination of John F. Kennedy shook the entire world and changed the course of history.

It just so happened, that on that day, November 22, 2003, it was the 40-year anniversary of that shot. We all knew that this was a very significant moment in the Spirit. As she prayed her prophetic prayer, she made a comparison: that a generation was coming to an end, and a change in the order of things, as we had known them, was happening, which she was relating to Israel and the United Methodist church.

After that time, Pastor Perry truly began to grow in his knowledge and understanding about the nation of Israel and the Jewish people. After Sherri died, this Israel understanding grew in many people, including myself. Even though I already had a deep love for Israel and the Jewish people because I had been studying about it for many years before I ever met her, she challenged me, because she put her faith into action. She taught me how to get beyond just learning and on to experiencing.

Another person that Sherri touched unknowingly, was our next pastor, Alan Ferguson. When Pastor Alan first came into the church, I remember vividly the day he came up to the *East River Ministries* office. He was amazed by the fact that we had this office concerning blessing and praying for Israel. I began to tell him the story of how it all came to be with Sherri's death.

Suddenly, he had a flashback. He remembered that he had known Sherri when they were both students at Asbury Seminary in Orlando! He knew very well those fiery blue eyes and her intense love for Israel. Over the course of three years, his understanding and love for Israel and the Jewish people has grown tremendously. He is a fervent prayer warrior for Israel and always remembers to lift them up in prayers in church.

Soon after my brother David's encounter with Sherri, he went to Israel and was teaching violin at Keshet Eilon, a world-renowned International Violin Mastercourse held in the Western Galilee. There he became acquainted with an Israeli man named Amnon Weinstein who is a violinmaker. Amnon has restored a collection of violins that had been played by Jewish people during the war. David told me the story of some of these violins and the people who played them.

Here is the story in David's own words:

> Some of [these violins] were even played in the concentration camps by the prisoners who were "lucky" enough to be chosen to play in the camp orchestra instead of going immediately to their deaths. As with many other things, the Nazis perverted the use of music. They felt they could use Jewish musicians for a practical purpose – to quell the fears of the people getting off the trains at places like Auschwitz-Birkenau. It was reasoned that the people arriving at the death camp would not believe there was any real danger there – after all, if there was music, even an orchestra in place to greet them at the train, the place they were arriving couldn't be all bad. Of course, the sad reality was that the Nazis were using music in this twisted way to deceive the people who were arriving at their place of death. One good thing came of this; the lives of the musicians who played in the Nazi's cruel orchestras were spared a little longer, even if only to watch their friends and loved ones march past them on the way to the gas chambers.

Today, Amnon uses these restored violins to restore hope into the hearts of mankind by producing concerts played on these violins at various locations around the world. One such concert was held at the Wailing Wall in Jerusalem on the 60th anniversary of the founding of the nation of Israel.

To make a very long story short, David and Amnon became friends. David, who is the Anne R. Belk Distinguished Professor of Music at University of North Carolina at Charlotte, is going to be bringing Amnon and the *Violins of Hope* project from Israel to the City of Charlotte at some point in the near future. It will be be the first time the project has been seen in this country.

Another fascinating part of Amnon's story is that he married Assi Bielski, the daughter of one of the famous Bielski brothers, who led a Jewish resistance to the Nazis during the war, in the forests of Byelorussia, which is told in the film *Defiance*. They hid Jewish people in the forest so they would be safe from being captured and taken to the concentration camps. The resistance the Bielskis led offered hope to many Jewish people during the Holocaust.

There is now an exhibit at the Florida Holocaust Museum which tells the story of the Bielski brothers. *The Violins of Hope* project in North Carolina will also include this exhibit.

There have been many other amazing things that God has done since Sherri said what she said to David all those years ago. He is traveling the world, playing his violin, and is constantly coming in contact with significant members of the Jewish communities in these places. One of these places is Le Chambon Sir Lignon in France. In this little village, more than five thousand Jewish people were hidden and saved from the Nazi's by the people of Le Chambon. These heroic people, descendants of the Hugenots, were under the direction of Pastor Andrew Trocme', a Protestant minister. They simply listened to God and their consciences and did the right thing in resisting the French government, who were aligned with Germany, and saved the lives of many Jewish people.

David recently did a violin concert in Le Chambon called, "The Power of Conscience," where he combined his musical talents, along with a spoken presentation, raising the questions, *Would we do the same thing today? Would we let our consciences over-ride our fears of a government or a system that is clearly in the wrong? Would we honor God and obey His higher laws, rather than fear man?*

I remember the day David called me to tell me about doing this concert. I was about to play in a concert myself, a reunion of our former violin teacher's students. We were at the rehearsal, and

David called. I had just recently been asking myself those very questions as mentioned above. "Would I have the courage to do the right thing today if I were called upon to help the Jewish people?" Just as I had been having these thoughts, he called and said, "Shishta (his pet Jewish name for me), you will never believe where I am headed!" And he told me the story of Le Chambon.

It turns out Sherri was right. It seems that even without his intentional effort, he is most defiantly "a part of this," and so are the rest of us.

The Hidden Surprise in the Old Wesley Hymnal

The clue I'd been waiting for all these years had finally happened. Not only was it a clue, but it was also a key, unlocking the very thing that I had suspected the whole time I have been in ministry. I had found out the truth about the Wesley brothers. They were early Zionists! They were Zionists long before there even was a homeland for the Jewish people.

How can that be? How could anyone have been a supporter of a homeland for the Jewish people in Israel long before there was a modern-day Israel? The answer was the same then as it is today; by studying God's word in its context. When we do this, we cannot come away with a theology in which Israel is replaced. We must see that God's covenants are unconditional, irrevocable and unchangeable. When He promised that Israel would someday be restored as a nation and a people, He meant it.

Supporting Israel is not about bringing politics into the church. Jesus predicted the destruction of Jerusalem, which happened just as He said. The Bible is clear about a long exile for the Jewish people, and then the return to the land. This also has happened. This Biblical way of looking at the modern-day Israel is called Zionism. It's about God's plan for the restoration and redemption of mankind. Jesus came through the Jewish people. Jerusalem is the throne of the Lord (Jeremiah 3:17).

God's grace is so amazing. He works in ways that we cannot even begin to understand or imagine. He does things beyond our wildest expectations. As we are walking with him day by day, seeking His will, His ways, His purposes, we can expect the wonderfully unexpected.

This was displayed to me in a marvelous way recently as I was sitting in my home office, just going about my daily work. Suddenly, an e-mail popped into my inbox. It was from my pastor, Alan Ferguson. It read:

Hi Hannah,

You may indeed have this information already. If not I think that it offers valuable insights and facts to support your\our efforts to rally the Alabama West Florida Conference of the UMC.

Many Blessings, Hannah

Pastor Alan

As casual as his words sounded, what they pointed to was not something I would toss to the side. Rather, what ensued in the next few minutes would have a profound ripple effect for the future. I can remember when Pastor Alan first came to our church. He commented to me that he hoped to somehow be a catalyst for change, a sentiment of which I shared. In my mind, his actions in the circumstances surrounding the sending of this e-mail would grant his heart's desire.

He later told me the story of why he sent me the information. He was in his office at church and was going through the mail. He was sifting through junk mail when he came to one that he almost tossed. He didn't recognize the organization it was from – *Final Frontier Ministries*. He didn't see anything on it that would indicate something which he had a connection. There was no United Methodist Church logo, no Israel flag or emblem, nothing that he recognized. However, the Holy Spirit wanted Him to open it, because he stopped, and for reasons he didn't understand at the time, he ripped into the envelope. The newsletter was from a man unknown to him, Avner Boskey, in Israel. If I had been at the church that day, I would have recognized the name because I had recently been at a concert in Panama City where he and his wife had performed Israeli songs. In fact, I know now that the reason the church had received the newsletter is probably because I had written a check from the *East River Ministries* account at Springfield United Methodist Church to Avner's ministry that day, and this put us on their mailing list.

When Pastor Alan opened the newsletter, the title at the top is what caught his attention. It was entitled "Aldersgate or Ichabod." For anyone who is a United Methodist, the term Aldersgate is very significant and well understood. Aldersgate is the name of the original church where John Wesley, the founder of the Methodists in England, had his "heartwarming experience." This is the place where his personal relationship with Jesus truly ignited. What had transpired from there became one of the greatest revivals the world had ever seen.

In contrast, the term "Ichabod" in Scripture means, "The glory has departed." These two words were very strong, and in Pastor Alan's mind, warranted a reading of the newsletter. What was the message of this letter written by Avner Boskey, a Messianic Jewish Pioneer in Israel?

Avner, who is obviously not a Methodist, captured the essence of what is happening within the bigger picture of the United Methodist Church. He took us Methodists back to the roots of our faith, both within our denomination, and also, our Biblical Jewish roots. He exposed the current belief of the United Methodist Church on the subject of Israel, which was something I had discovered several years ago and was the reason why I had been writing resolutions to change things. His point in writing the newsletter was to show us what was really in the hearts of our founders, John and Charles Wesley. Charles was John's brother who wrote over 6,000 hymns during the days of the "Great Awakening."

This was a fact that was well-known throughout church history. Methodists and other denominations have sung Charles' familiar hymns for many years. Tunes like "O For a Thousand Tongues," and "And Can it Be That I Should Gain," as well as "Hark the Herald Angels Sing," are songs that have been on the lips of all of us who have grown up in the church.

The point of his letter, however, was not only to expose where we have gone as a denomination in coming against Israel, but to show how far away we really are from the vision of the Wesleys, our founders, not to mention, the Scripture.

I had suspected John Wesley's love for the Jewish people based on a few words found in a book I had read. What I read, however, in the newsletter sent to me by Pastor Alan, sent me into such joy I could hardly contain it. Avner Boskey displayed parts of two out of three of Charles Wesley's hymns that prove beyond a shadow of a doubt that the Wesley's were ardent Zionists.[11]

In other words, John and Charles believed that the Jewish people were to return in a physical sense to their homeland, receive the Jewish Messiah (Jesus) and would be a light to the nations! Consider the implications of these hymns which are found in the very oldest of the 1762 Methodist Hymnals, "A Collection of Hymns for the Use of the People Called Methodists," written by Charles and later edited by John.[12]

Almighty God of Love

Almighty God of love,
set up the attracting sign,
And summon whom thou dost approve
for messengers divine,

From favoured Abraham's seed,
the new apostles choose,
In isles and continents to spread,
the dead-reviving news,

---

11 http://www.davidstent.org/newsletters/2010/July%205%202010.htm
12 http://www.wesley-fellowship.org.uk/Zionist_Hymn.html

Operation Olive Branch

Them, snatched out of the flame,
through every nation send,
The true Messiah to proclaim,
the universal friend;

That all the God unknown,
may learn of Jews to adore,
And see Thy glory in Thy Son,
till time shall be no more.

O that the chosen band,
might now their bretheren bring,
And gathered out of every land,
present to Zion's King!

Of all the ancient race,
not one be left behind,
But each impelled by secret grace,
His way to Canaan find.

We know it must be done,
for God hath spoke the word:
All Israel shall the Saviour own,
To their first state restored;

Rebuilt by his command,
Jerusalem shall rise;
Her temple on Moriah stand
again, and touch the skies.

Send then thy servants forth,
to call the Hebrews home;
From East, and West, and South, and North,
Let all the wanderers come;

Where'er in lands unknown
The fugitives remain,
Bid every creature help them
on Thy holy mount to gain.

> An offering to their God,
> there let them all be seen,
> Sprinkled with water and with blood,
> in soul and body clean;
>
> With Israel's myriads sealed,
> let all the nations meet,
> And show the mystery fulfilled,
> Thy family complete![13]

Praying Softly for Jerusalem

> FATHER of faithful Abraham,
> hear our earnest suit for Abraham's seed!
> Justly they claim the softest prayer from us…
>
> Come then, Thou great Deliverer, come!
> The veil from Jacob's heart remove;
> Receive Thy ancient people home!
>
> That, quickened by Thy dying love,
> The world may their reception find
> life from the dead for all mankind.

(Father of faithful Abraham, words & music Charles Wesley, 1762, based on Romans 11:15-27)[14]

I, personally, would love to see these hymns restored and to be sung in churches, just as the other many beloved songs have been sung. Perhaps if we begin helping this generation see where we came from, our denomination will take a much more active role in God's plan of restoration for the nations.

---

13 http://www.davidstent.org/newsletters/2010/July%205%202010.htm
14 http://www.ccel.org/w/wesley/hymn/jwg04/jwg0451.html

The Note in A Bottle Mystery

To understand this next mystery, you must go back and read the previous stories in this book about my friend Sherri. Those stories lay the foundation for this final chapter. Supposing you have read them, I will proceed, first with my side of this story and then Sherri's.

When I first met Sherri, she was a bundle of God-inspired energy. She was full of passion and zeal for Jesus, and also for her mission in life, which was ministering to the Jewish people and Israel. Since this also happened to be a very strong passion of mine as well, we connected on that level, even though at times she was difficult to understand.

She had so much going on in her head at one time, and she would get so excited as she talked, that sometimes she would verbalize things in a bit of a jumbled sort of way. I once heard her manner of presentation described as "scrambled eggs." It was all very good stuff, but not always easy to grasp because of the depth. As time went on, she became more understandable, at least to me. I believe this was, in part, because God was speaking to me in similar ways, and I could pick up on key words, phrases and Bible verses that she would use. After she died, these began to make more and more sense, as I read through some of the things she had written.

As I have continued on this journey, it has been a progressive revelation to me from the Lord, uncovering the mystery of my Jewish roots. I still have many of Sherri's writings, and at first, they didn't make too much sense. However, it is now a different story. As I read her words, and put them together with the things I have learned, and also, the things I remember her saying to me, it is truly a mystery unfolding.

It seems that God always lets me find things that she had written, right in the moment I need them. This last chapter of the book was revealed to me in this mysterious way, and quite unexpectedly.

A mutual friend of Sherri's and mine, Dalia, recently met me for a birthday breakfast. We have been doing this for years as our birthdays are September 14th and 15th, respectively. Those dates were so significant in 2004, as Hurricane Ivan, the hurricane that would ultimately be responsible for Sherri's death, was making landfall. Sherri died on the morning of the eve of Rosh Hashanah, 2004, in the early morning hours of Sept. 15th.

I remember that one of the first and ongoing stories that Sherri told me was concerning Marcia, a Jewish woman. I also heard Sherri say many times throughout our friendship that she was going to write a book about all the things God had shown her about the Jewish people. As my life became connected with hers more and more, her stories became my stories, so sometimes she actually would talk about the book as if we were writing it together. At that time, I never really felt connected with it, but God has changed all of that.

I can clearly remember that twenty-four hour period in 2004 on Yom Kippur, when I had just heard that Sherri's plane was missing. During that time, God spoke to my heart to continue this Israel ministry. The name that God had given Sherri in the beginning for her part in the ministry had been "Bittersweet Seeds." I'm not totally sure of all of her reasons for naming it that, but I do remember a part of the reason, and it had to do with the suffering of Jesus, having to be a seed that died, so He could rise again and give life to the world. Sherri also came to find out that she would have to endure suffering to carry out her ministry, and she wound up being a bittersweet seed herself. After she died, many people, including myself, seemed to wake up in their understanding of the action required when one is in a ministry to God's chosen people, Israel.

The Lord later gave me the name for my part of the ministry, which was *East River*. Besides telling me to continue the ministry, that day of Yom Kippur 2004, He also confirmed to me that I was to write a book. It has taken me six years to actually understand what it was I was supposed to write. Now I know that I was to write my own stories of how I came to understand this great mystery of uncovering our Jewish roots. What I didn't realize was how much Sherri's stories would intersect my stories.

The year that this book was written, 2010, Dalia and I were ten days late for our birthday get-together. The year Sherri died in 2004, we did not find out the plane was missing until ten days after our birthdays, so this was, again, an anniversary of sorts. As I was having breakfast with Dalia, we were reminiscing about Sherri. This seems to happen whenever Dalia and I get together, particularly at this time of year. We usually wind up laughing over "Sherri-isms."

For example, like the way she would get intensely excited whenever she would see something in one of us that made her spiritual antennas go up. She was always on a mission for God, which inevitably involved Israel in the bigger picture, and she would see our gifts and talents and how they might be best used for this purpose. If you were the "chosen one" on a particular day, she would say in her loveable and affirming, but deadly serious voice, "You know you're a part of this, don't you?" And she would pat you on the arm or something, in a kind of motherly way. There was always a place in the Kingdom for all God's children.

As we were leaving that day, Dalia had something for me in her trunk. It was a box full of Hebrew books and maps that she had bought years ago at a garage sale. She had not used them and had decided to give them to me. I joyfully received this box of treasures, because I love to study Jewish roots. When I got home, I began to go through the box.

Besides the books and maps, there was a set of papers stapled together. As soon as I started to read the words, I knew they were Sherri's. Did Dalia forget to tell me that she had put this story of Sherri's in the box? I could hardly believe what I was seeing! She

hadn't mentioned it to me. Later, I found out that she had stuck it in the box a while back and yes, she had forgotten to mention it. She could just as easily have left it out of the box. It was really the only paper in it. Everything else was a book or a map. This was God's sovereign hand at work, keeping a thing hidden until the exact moment that it was to be revealed. He is very detail oriented. I used to say this many years ago, and it is time to pull it out again: "God is so accurate!"

It was when I read the last line of the story, that I knew that I was to include it. I was absolutely astounded as I read through these very familiar words that Sherri had told me many times. It was different, somehow, reading her words on paper. As I continued to read, I was so amazed at the timing of all of this! The last line really tied everything together, and I mean everything!

We had talked about writing this book so many times however, it was mostly her at the time. Now, the entire subject matter was coming together in this last line. It read, "Through prophetic insight and action, we the Gentiles, can embrace our roots and **together complete the last chapter in the book.**" When I read those words, I was amazed, astounded and full of joy! I realized that this would literally be the last chapter in the book, *Operation Olive Branch,* and it would be Sherri and me, writing it together!

The story Sherri had written was about Marcia, the Jewish woman. It was written in Sherri's sort-of "scrambled eggs" style, but I had heard it enough in the past, that now, I could make sense of the whole thing, filling in the blanks as I read. For the sake of clarification, I have decided not to use her exact words, but to paraphrase as I write her amazing story.

I will now tell you in my paraphrased version what was on the paper I found in the box. This is quite incredible. I hope you will enjoy this story as much as I did.

SHERRI'S STORY

First was an explanation of how Sherri had come about the information I was about to read. She was trying to convey the experience and a vision that she had discerned while in Miami one summer. She had gifts from the Holy Spirit that enabled her to see and sense deep meanings in given situations that people might overlook if they weren't tuned in to the right frequency. She had written this chapter for her book to explain how the Holy Spirit worked in her and through her with these gifts and to explain something concerning her understanding about God's chosen people, the Jews.

One day, the Lord impressed upon her to call Marcia, a Jewish woman who lived in Miami, and ask to stay with her while she was attending college. Right after she hung up the receiver, she was reminded by the Lord of a Scripture she had read the night before that she had felt was particularly for her. It was Matthew 8:6. "Lord, my servant is lying at home paralyzed, dreadfully tormented."

In awe, she remembered that Marcia was one-half paralyzed. One week later, she called Marcia, and found her to be in torment. She had learned of a growth in her lung that had to be removed. The week after, she informed Sherri that the growth was malignant.

After Sherri arrived in Miami and went to the doctor with Marcia, something connected between them when she showed Sherri a picture of a bottle with a note in it. The picture was in a magazine she was looking at in the doctor's office. The bottle had washed up on the shore, and the caption to the magazine article read, "A Message from the Father from Years Ago."

Sherri's discernment began to kick into gear at this point. She realized that Marcia had a stagnant life. Her faith as a Jewish person was weak, and what little faith she had in the past in Yeshua/Jesus as her Savior was also weak. Apparently, Marcia had previously had some sort of encounter with Christianity, but it seemed like she didn't know how to walk with Him, and her faith was not strong.

Marcia also doubted Yeshua's love for His chosen people, Israel, and how this love is shown through Christians like Sherri. This is the case with many Jewish people who have experienced horrible atrocities at the hands of others, as well as people who called themselves Christians. Marcia couldn't understand what Sherri realized, that it is the Christian's duty to help expand the Jews' faith and understanding toward Yeshua, (which was now a rising movement), and for the Jews to teach the Christians about our roots.

She also discovered how lonely Marcia was when she realized that her daughter lived in one side of the house, while Marcia lived almost constantly sitting in one chair on the other. To remedy this situation, Sherri spent time with her, teaching her of the Spirit and Yeshua, while Marcia taught her of Jewish customs.

One of these customs was concerning the blue thread on the tallit (prayer shawl) used by the priests. One thing Marcia taught her was that a certain snail used to make blue dye that was used in the tallit, was just rediscovered after two-thousand years.

Prior to Marcia's lung surgery, the Lord had led Sherri to Matthew 8:7, where Jesus said, "I will come and heal him." As Sherri helped Marcia get into bed, she laid her back onto the pillows, and Marcia accepted that healing from Yeshua, confessing her sin, saying, "Yes," to God the Father and Yeshua.

Sherri sensed Marcia's general faith was weak to believe that a healing would actually come forth. Although she had agreed in faith for the healing from God, Sherri felt that Marcia was putting more faith in the doctor's ability to make her well, than in what God would do. However, as she left the hospital after her surgery, she was exclaiming, "I am the miracle on this floor!"

At age 53, she had survived lung surgery, even with having two aneurysms in her head. The very day that Sherri left, Marcia's lymph node test came in clear. "Like an ending in a chapter of a book," (Sherri's words) Marcia was healed. Now, she realized how gracious God had been to save her life!

Through this experience, Yeshua made it clear to Sherri that we are to feed His people manna (spiritual food which can only be understood by the Spirit).

Sherri said in her story:

> He is the branch that holds the roots and the top of the tree together, the lifeline to both. The top of the tree cannot grow without the roots, our past, Israel. The roots are paralyzed and stagnant without the top branches of new growth, the church's reaching out to give new life and to heal. We need each other. The reality that God loves His chosen people, the Jews, rings forth through this testimony as proof.

He loved Marcia so much that He sent Sherri all the way to Miami to minister to her in her time of need.

As she reflected on this experience, Sherri was able to see how Yeshua worked through her during critical circumstances as she reached forth to Marcia, and she groped for that lifeline, that blue thread. Prior to leaving for Miami and while interceding for Marcia, Sherri had a vision of a blue thread on the tallit of Yeshua.

In the vision, Sherri was that thread, suspended and hanging, yet able to enter into His secret place, under the shadow of His presence, symbolized by the tallit. Luke 8:44 tells the story of the woman with the issue of blood, reaching for the hem of Jesus' garment. This was actually the tzitzit, the fringe on the corners of the tallit, which represents the Word of God. The woman in the story was reaching for the Truth. She was reaching for the Word of God. She was reaching for her healing. She was reaching for Yeshua/Jesus, her Messiah, and her faith in Him is what healed her and made her whole.

Sherri remembered interceding for both Marcia and for her people. She opened her eyes as she was praying and saw her own hand holding Marcia's hand, the old and the new, the Gentile and the Jew, and felt the cleansing fire between. Tears were flowing. His healing presence was there. As she let go to reach for a tissue, Sherri saw Marcia's hand groping and reaching out for hers. Marcia was that woman with the issue of blood. Israel was that woman with the issue of blood. It all came together in that moment.

When Sherri returned home and came into her house, there was a surprise waiting for her. These were the kinds of things that happened to her and to all of us as we are walking with Him by the power of His Spirit. She looked up and noticed a postcard taped to the kitchen cabinet. On it was a picture of a bottle with a message inside, washed up on the shore, similar to the one she had seen in the doctor's office. It's caption simply read, "Missed."

From that time forward, Sherri believed, and I believe as well, that what Yeshua (Jesus) said through the symbolism of the message in the bottle, was this:

> The message of the gospel has gone around the world, but we have overlooked His people and His land Israel. We, the Gentiles, must reach out and help those of the Jewish faith find healing and their way home. Through prophetic insight and action, we the Gentiles can embrace our roots, and together complete the last chapter in the book.

Afterword

God's Mysterious Plan for the Fruit of the Nations

Everyone has an opinion about something. We are diverse individuals and our thinking has been influenced by many different factors. If we are Bible-believing Christians, our thinking should be influenced by the word of God. We shouldn't pick and choose Scriptures here and there that conform to our ideals. The context of the whole of Scripture should shape our ideologies. This way of thinking is applying the Logos – the whole and complete word of God, and allowing it to transform us into the image of Jesus, the Messiah.

I have been a member of the United Methodist Church for twenty-three years. During that time, I have met many wonderful people who have influenced my life. some of the most significant people in my life are United Methodists. However, as much as I love these people, God's word has been my biggest influence. I began to study the scriptures early in my Christian walk. My theologies were formed based on what I was seeing in Scripture and not necessarily always what I was being taught by a denomination.

One of the first concepts that I began to learn as I was studying scripture was God's dealings with the nation of Israel and the Jewish people. It all began with Abram, later know as Abraham. God told him in Genesis 12:1-3,

> *...Go forth from your country, and from your relatives, and from your father's house, to the land which I will show you; and I will make you a great nation, and I will bless you, and make your name great; and so you shall be a blessing; and I will bless those*

who bless you, and the one who curses you I will curse. And in you all the families of the earth will be blessed.

The promise was repeated to his son Isaac in Genesis17:19.

But God said, 'No, but Sarah your wife will bear you a son, and you shall call his name Isaac; and I will establish My covenant with him for an everlasting covenant for his descendants after him.'

Verses 20-21 makes it clear that the promise that was given to Abraham and Isaac was not the promise that was given to Ishmael, Abraham's son by Hagar. God said,

As for Ishmael, I have heard you; behold I will bless him, and will make him fruitful and will multiply him exceedingly. He shall become the father of twelve princes, and I will make him a great nation. But My covenant I will establish with Isaac, whom Sarah will bear to you at this season next year.

To take it one step further, the promise was given to Isaac's son Jacob, who's name God changed to Israel in Genesis 35:10-12. God said to him,

...Your name is Jacob; you shall no longer be called Jacob, but Israel shall be your name. Thus He called him Israel. God also said to him, 'I am God Almighty; Be fruitful and multiply; a nation and a company of nations shall come from you, and kings shall come forth from you. The land which I gave to Abraham and Isaac, I will give it to you, and I will give the land to your descendants after you.

In my Bible, (NASB) Psalm105:6-15 is titled, "THE LORD'S WONDERFUL WORKS IN BEHALF OF ISRAEL." It reads as follows:

O seed of Abraham, His servant, O sons of Jacob, His chosen ones! He is the LORD our God; His judgments are in all the earth. He has remembered His covenant forever, the word which He commanded to a thousand generations. The covenant which He made with Abraham, and His oath to Isaac. Then He confirmed it to Jacob for a statute, To Israel as an everlasting covenant, saying, "To you I will give the land of Caanan as the portion of your inheritance," when they were only a few in number, very few, and strangers in it. And they wandered about from nation to nation, from one kingdom to another people. He permitted no man to oppress them, and He reproved kings for their sakes; "do not touch My anointed ones, and do My prophets no harm.

This is the foundation upon which rests the establishment of the nation of Israel and the chosen people of God, the Jews. If a country, a church or an individual takes the Bible seriously and seeks to live according to God's word, there can be no denying from these Scriptures alone that God has established forever His covenant with Abraham, Isaac and Jacob (or Israel). The land belongs to them and through God's plan of the land belonging to Israel, all the nations of the world will be blessed. God's plan is big enough for all nations and all people.

There is a kingdom order of priority that must be followed in order for this plan to be fulfilled. It is the "Jew First" principle that is found throughout scripture. One of the first scriptures I ever learned as a young believer in Messiah Jesus was Romans 1:16. "For I am not ashamed of the gospel, for it is the power of God for salvation to everyone who believes, to the Jew first and also to the Greek." I believe this means several things. The Jews were indeed the first to receive the gospel through Jesus when He was on the earth; In fact, Jesus said that He had come only for the lost sheep of the house of Israel. However, I also believe that God is establishing a principal that all of us are to follow. Salvation is for the Jew first, because of His promises and covenants with them that He will fulfill. He has a plan and a purpose for His people. All the nations of the world will be blessed through them. We are to keep them first in prayers, always lifting them up first and as a priority, to the Father. In doing this, we will reap the fruit of the nations.

Yet, there are many countries, churches and individuals who seem to be blind to these Scriptures, and the truth about the Jewish people and the nation of Israel. How can this be, when it is so plain? This is not a covenant that ended with a generation. This is a perpetual, everlasting covenant that goes on forever. What God said to Abraham, Isaac and Jacob, He says today, to their descendants and to all of us who will listen.

We have no control over how God makes His choices and His plans. All we can do is accept it. If something is plainly revealed in Scripture, why would we fight against it? He has chosen Israel and is not finished with them. He is fulfilling His purposes in the earth through this nation. They gave us our Jewish Messiah, Jesus. He loves His people, and it says in Jeremiah 3:17 that Jerusalem is the throne of the Lord. Out of all the places in the world He could have chosen, He chose Israel, with Jerusalem as it's capital as a place for His promises to be fulfilled.

Since He is God, the question we must ask ourselves is this: Do we get with God's program so that we can work alongside Him in what He is doing?

Appendix A:

Poll on the Middle East Crisis

POLL ON THE MIDDLE EAST CRISIS
ALABAMA WEST FLORIDA ANNUAL CONFERENCE 2009

1. Do you believe the Holocaust really happened?_____
2. Do you believe that a modern-day Holocaust of Jews and/or Christians could happen today? _____
3. Based on what you believe the Bible to say, does Israel have claim to the whole land, or should there be a two-state solution?_____
4. Are you aware of the official United Methodist Church's stand regarding the land of Israel as stated in the Book of Resolutions?_____
5. When God said in Genesis 12:3, "I will bless those who bless you and curse those who curse you" Do you believe that this is still relevant for today?_____
6. Do you believe we are called to pray for the peace of Jerusalem? _____
7. Can man bring true and lasting peace? _____

Appendix B:

Resolution Regarding Israel and Replacement Theology

Whereas, while we, as members of the Alabama West Florida Conference, acknowledge that God loves all people, and that His promises apply in a spiritual sense to all who receive His free gift of eternal salvation through Jesus, we reject all forms of Replacement Theology, which subscribes to the thinking that the church has replaced natural Israel in the plans of God, or that God is finished with Israel, and

Whereas, Psalm 105:6-15 addresses natural Israel in stating, "O seed of Abraham, His servant, O sons of Jacob, His chosen ones!, He is the Lord our God; His judgments are in all the earth." The verse goes on to exemplify the sustainability of God's promise to natural Israel in saying: "He has remembered His covenant forever, the word which He commanded *to a thousand generations*, the covenant which He made with Abraham and His oath to Isaac. Then He confirmed it to Jacob for a statute, to Israel as *an everlasting covenant, saying, 'to you I will give the land of Canaan as the portion of your inheritance,'* when they were only a few men in number, very few and strangers in it." The verse goes on to speak of Israel's Diaspora (being scattered to the nations), although not without God's divine hand being on them, as indicated: "And they wandered about from nation to nation, from one kingdom to another people. He permitted no man to oppress them, and He reproved kings for their sakes: 'Do not touch My anointed ones, and do My prophets no harm'" and

Whereas, in regards to the faithfulness of God's word concerning His promises to Israel, He makes this *conditional* promise in Jeremiah 31:35-36, which states, "Thus says the Lord, who gives the sun for light by day, and the fixed order of the moon and the stars for light by night, who stirs up the sea so that its waves roar;

the Lord of hosts is His name; *if* this fixed order departs from before Me, declares the Lord, *then* the offspring of Israel also shall cease from being a nation before Me forever," (meaning he upholds his promises to them as he upholds his creation), and

Whereas, to further illustrate God's adversity to the nations who are against natural Israel, Zechariah 2:8 says, "For thus says the Lord of hosts, "After glory He has sent me against the nations which plunder you, for he who touches you, touches the apple of His eye," and

Whereas, according to Psalm 122:6 we are commanded to "Pray for the peace of Jerusalem,"

Therefore, be it resolved, that we as the Bible-believing people of the Alabama West Florida Conference, accept God's everlasting covenant with the nation of Israel. We stand together in support of the nation of Israel, and promise to make it a priority, both individually and collectively, to pray for the peace of Jerusalem, and the well-being of the nation of Israel, and for revelation, and for God's perfect will to be done.

Submitted by:
Hannah May
Director of *East River Ministries*
850-890-0649
yngsmsmm@aol.com

Appendix C:

Resolution Regarding the Jewish People and Anti-Semitism

Whereas we, the Alabama West Florida Conference, recognize that for hundreds of years, the church has, in many cases, not acknowledged our Jewish roots, due to the separation by some of our forefathers from everything Jewish due, in part, to misunderstanding, and

Whereas, we therefore affirm our Jewish roots and seek fresh understanding of the common heritage that we have with the chosen people of the God of Abraham, Isaac and Jacob, and

Whereas, we thank the Jewish people for their many contributions to mankind, in the way of industry, innovations, inventions, medicine, agriculture, the arts, etc., In particular, we show gratitude to them for giving us, as well as preserving, our Bible, written by the inspiration of God by the hand of mostly Jewish writers, both old and new testaments, and most especially, for being the nation that God chose to give us our shared Messiah, Jesus (Yeshua), and

Whereas, we recognize that God chose the nation of Israel and Jerusalem as the focal point for all of history, in the past, present and for the future, and

Whereas, we also recognize that there are many in our world today who, still, unbelievably, deny the holocaust ever happened. We, therefore, do not join in agreement with this, and earnestly seek to keep the remembrance of it ever before us, so that it cannot ever happen again, and

Therefore, be it resolved that, as the people of the Alabama West Florida Conference, we reject all forms of anti-Semitism, and earnestly seek to stand in repentance for some of those of the Christian faith, and some of our forefathers, who in ages past and also the present, have perpetrated horrific deeds against the Jewish people. This has been done in various ways, either through actions, apathy, ignorance, or unloving words. We pray that persecution of God's chosen people will never happen again, and

Therefore, be it further resolved that we sincerely hope this will open the way for tearing down walls between us, which in many cases, have kept the Jewish people from hearing the Good News of the gospel, which according to Romans 1:16 is "to the Jew first, and also to the Greek" (Nations,), and

Therefore, we also resolve to look for tangible ways to be a blessing to the Jewish people as well as the land and the people of Israel, showing unconditional love and support. We believe in being a blessing, not just in words, but in actions.

Submitted by:
Hannah May
Director of *East River Ministries*
850-890-0649
yngsmsmm@aol.com

Appendix D:

East River Ministries Twelve Tribes Small Groups

This program is in memory of Sherri Bomback and family.

Begin with (at least) 12 hosts/hostesses who will begin a small group in their home, and invite (at least) 12 people to become part of that group. These small groups can be anywhere in the country or even the world! Each small group will meet every month (12 times per year).

THE PURPOSE OF THESE 12 SMALL GROUPS

1. To pray for the salvation and restoration of each of the 12 tribes of Israel.
2. To pray for their release from the four corners of the earth as they make Aliyah (immigrate) to Israel, fulfilling Bible prophecy.
3. To form cohesiveness and bring focus and unity within *East River Ministries*.
4. To enjoy a monthly fellowship within a small group.
5. To develop and strengthen a love for the land and people of Israel and to increase in knowledge and understanding of why Israel matters to God and us.
6. To love, pray for and encourage each other for healing and restoration as individual needs may arise.

HOW THE SMALL GROUPS (TRIBES) WORK

Each of the twelve small groups will be designated a name of one of the twelve tribes with which they will be identified.

Each of the twelve small groups, when they gather each month, will focus their discussion and prayers on one of the twelve tribes, until at the end of the year they will have covered all twelve tribes. Each month will be designated for a particular tribe, that all of the groups will be focused on. A general outline will be provided by *East River Ministries* to facilitate the discussion and prayer.

The Twelve Tribes are:

Reuben, Simeon, Levi, Judah, Issachar, Zebulun, Joseph, Benjamin, Dan, Naphtali, Gad, and Asher.

Leader/Facilitator

There should be a person who will lead or facilitate the discussion and prayer each month. This can be the same person each time, or a different person who will be decided upon at each meeting for the next month.

Scribes and Praise Reports

Within the groups, someone will be designated for that month, or ongoing, as "scribe" who will write a praise report of that particular meeting and e-mail it to *East River Ministries* (yngsmsmm@aol.com). This should be done immediately, while it is still fresh in mind of that scribe. These monthly praise reports will be invaluable as we come together at the end of the year to share what God has done within each group.

Freedom within the groups

There is freedom for individuals to visit or switch to various groups as they feel comfortable. The host/hostess is encouraged to invite others along the way. These are not closed groups, but open and welcoming any who would want to participate at any time. Individual prayer is encouraged for personal needs. There should be freedom within the groups to be led by the Holy Spirit as His plans are not always our plans. Since the true theme of these gatherings is "restoration", it is important to pray, not only for the Tribes of Israel in a literal sense, but also for all those who want prayer. We suggest that you do not take the time to make lists, but simply if a need is verbalized and the Holy Spirit is confirms, then stop and pray for that person. We are believing God to do great and mighty things, and for His blessings to flow within Israel, as well as within the lives of those who participate.

LOVE OFFERINGS

Those who attend may want to bring a $12 per month offering as part of the 144,000 campaign (see www.eastriverministries.com), but not required. A love offering for *East River Ministries* may be taken by passing an offering basket.

MENUS AND GATHERING ARRANGEMENTS

Each host/hostess may decide their own menus for each month, whether it will be covered dish and every member of the group bringing an item to share, or they may want to prepare all the food themselves. Location of the meetings is also decided by the group, whether stationary or rotated to various homes. The important thing is that they do meet together each month. The day and time of their meeting should be consistent and allow for re-scheduling if necessary.

SCHEDULE AND HANUKKAH PARTY

The small groups will begin in January, and end in December, all coming together for a Hanukkah party. The theme of Hanukkah is about "restoration", because it is a celebration of the temple being restored. Each of the "tribes" will be responsible for decorating a table for their tribe, and will share insights and experiences from their twelve months of meetings. If a particular "tribe" from another area of the country is too far away that they cannot all attend, perhaps a representative(s) could be sent, or they could have their own Hanukkah party with the Twelve Tribes theme.

Appendix E:

Find the Hidden Symbols on the Cover

Messianic Seal – This symbol was originally found on some very old pottery dating back to the time of the disciples in the upper room just after Jesus ascended to heaven. The tail of the Christian fish symbol joins with the base of the Jewish Menorah, forming the Star of David in the center. This has become an increasingly used expression of the "One New Man" from Ephesians 2:15, which is Jew and Gentile, one in the Messiah.

The Dove – Universally recognized as a symbol of peace, dating back to the story of Noah's ark. When the dove returned after the flood with an olive branch in its mouth, Noah recognized that the waters had receded and they had entered a new time of peace with God. The dove with the olive branch in its mouth represents for many an extension of peace and goodwill, particularly in the Middle East crisis, as man tries countless ways to achieve this peace. However, the dove also represents the Holy Spirit, who came down from heaven and lit on Jesus at His baptism. The Trinity, (Father, Son and Holy Spirit), are beautifully seen in this passage in Matthew 3:13-17. We know that true and lasting peace in the Middle East and anywhere else can only come through the Prince of Peace, Jesus, as we yield to His divine order.

Hebrew Letters – Aleph, Kaf, and Dalet - This Hebrew word is "Echad", meaning "One". This word is found prominently in the "Shema" from Deuteronomy 6:4, "Hear O Israel, the Lord our God, the Lord is ONE." This is precisely why many Jewish people have difficulty with God's greatest mystery, the Trinity, because they are seeing only the separate components. However, understanding the Trinity helps us to better understand that Father, Son, and Holy Spirit are the "One" referred to in this passage. God, the perfect Father, sent His only, perfect Son, with Him from eternity, to die for the sins of the whole world. (Micah 5:2) Jesus then sent the Holy Spirit to indwell believers so that we would all be one with Him. (John 17:22)

Cross and Flame – Representing the Holy Spirit who descended in the form of flames of fire, alongside the cross. This has been meaningful to me as a United Methodist, helping me to understand that we were birthed in the fires of the revival of John and Charles Wesley. Much of the work of East River Ministries has been focused on changing the resolutions of the Methodist Church on Israel.

The Number 7 – God's number of perfection and completion. This is the only hidden picture that was not intentionally placed there, but I believe God wanted it seen. All things are complete in Him, and we are only complete as we put our faith and trust in His perfect sacrifice.

"Y" – Shaped Branch – This is symbolic of the passages in Romans 9-11, which explains in detail how Israel the natural olive branch was broken off, and we Gentiles, the wild olive branch, were grafted into the rich root of the olive tree. Those branches who were broken off will be grafted back in, and we will all be one in the Messiah. It is also representative of the two sticks in one hand from Ezekiel 37:15-28, the two "houses" of Israel, coming together in the end. This is the whole house of Israel, fully restored.

Cross and Flame – Representing the holy Spirit who descended in the form of flames of fire, alongside the cross. This has been meaningful to me as a United Methodist, helping me to understand that we were birthed in the fires of the revival of

John and Charles Wesley. Much of the work of *East River Ministries* has been focused on changing the resolutions regarding Israel in the United Methodist Church.

More from Energion Publications

Personal Study

The Jesus Paradigm	$17.99
Finding My Way in Christianity	$16.99
When People Speak for God	$17.99
Holy Smoke, Unholy Fire	$14.99
Not Ashamed of the Gospel	$12.99
Evidence for the Bible	$16.99
Christianity and Secularism	$16.99
What's In A Version?	$12.99
Christian Archy	$9.99
Ultimate Allegiance	$9.99
The Messiah and His Kingdom to Come	$19.99 (B&W)

Christian Living

Daily Devotions of Ordinary People – Extraordinary God	$19.99
Directed Paths	$7.99
Grief: Finding the Candle of Light	$8.99
I Want to Pray	$7.99
Soup Kitchen for the Soul	$12.99

Bible Study

Learning and Living Scripture	$12.99
To the Hebrews: A Participatory Study Guide	$9.99
Revelation: A Participatory Study Guide	$9.99
The Gospel According to St. Luke: A Participatory Study Guide	$8.99
Ephesians: A Participatory Study Guide	$9.99
Identifying Your Gifts and Service: Small Group Edition	$12.99
Why Four Gospels?	$11.99

Theology

God's Desire for the Nations	$18.99

Fiction

Megabelt	$12.99

Generous Quantity Discounts Available
Dealer Inquiries Welcome
Energion Publications
P.O. Box 841
Gonzalez, FL 32560
Website: http://energionpubs.com
Phone: (850) 525-3916

CPSIA information can be obtained at www.ICGtesting.com
225772LV00003B/1/P